KNOCKING
ON
WINDOWS

ALSO BY
Jeannine Atkins

FINDING WONDERS:
Three Girls Who Changed Science

GRASPING MYSTERIES:
Girls Who Loved Math

GREEN PROMISES:
Girls Who Loved the Earth

HIDDEN POWERS:
Lise Meitner's Call to Science

STONE MIRRORS:
*The Sculpture and Silence
of Edmonia Lewis*

Jeannine Atkins

KNOCKING ON WINDOWS

A MEMOIR

atheneum

New York   Amsterdam/Antwerp   London
Toronto   Sydney/Melbourne   New Delhi

atheneum

An imprint of Simon & Schuster Children's Publishing Division
1230 Avenue of the Americas, New York, New York 10020

This work is a memoir. It reflects the author's present recollections of her experiences over a
period of years. Certain names and other characteristics have been changed.

Text © 2025 by Jeannine Atkins
Jacket photography © 2025 by Getty Stock
Thistle photo by Bloom Images
Bee photo by Don Mason
Jacket design by Debra Sfetsios-Conover
All rights reserved, including the right of reproduction in whole or in part in any form.
Atheneum logo is a trademark of Simon & Schuster, LLC.
For information about special discounts for bulk purchases, please contact Simon & Schuster
Special Sales at 1-866-506-1949 or business@simonandschuster.com.
Simon & Schuster strongly believes in freedom of expression and stands against censorship in
all its forms. For more information, visit BooksBelong.com.
The Simon & Schuster Speakers Bureau can bring authors to your live event. For more
information or to book an event, contact the Simon & Schuster Speakers Bureau at
1-866-248-3049 or visit our website at www.simonspeakers.com.
Interior design by Irene Metaxatos
The text for this book was set in Haboro.
Manufactured in the United States of America
First Edition
10 9 8 7 6 5 4 3 2 1
Library of Congress Cataloging-in-Publication Data
Names: Atkins, Jeannine, 1953- author.
Title: Knocking on windows : a memoir / Jeannine Atkins.
Description: First edition. | New York : Atheneum Books for Young Readers, 2025. | Audience:
Ages 14 and up | Summary: "Acclaimed author Jeannine Atkins tells her story in this brave and
powerful memoir-in-verse about memory, healing, and finding her voice as a writer."–Provided
by publisher.
Identifiers: LCCN 2024042253 (print) | LCCN 2024042254 (ebook) | ISBN 9781665977548
(hardcover) | ISBN 9781665977562 (ebook)
Subjects: LCSH: Atkins, Jeannine, 1953- | Women authors, American–Biography. | Sexual
assault–United States–Biography. | LCGFT: Autobiographies. | Poetry. | Creative nonfiction.
Classification: LCC PS3601.T4885 Z46 2025 (print) | LCC PS3601.T4885 (ebook) |
DDC 813/.6 [B]–dc23/eng/20241011
LC record available at https://lccn.loc.gov/2024042253
LC ebook record available at https://lccn.loc.gov/2024042254

To the faculty and therapists who helped guide me
through my college years, especially
Julia Demmin, Jean Matlack, Margo Culley,
John Clayton, and Andrew Fetler.
My writing is shaped by gratitude for them,
other generous people who believed in me and
my work, and readers I've never met.
Dear friends: let's look out for each other.

PART I

Edges

Tales of Long Ago

Night darkens the window to mirror.
My childhood bedroom looks unfamiliar.
A sheet of asbestos was set over the radiator
back when I was small and we didn't know
it was dangerous. It's covered with a doily
and small china animals: a Scottie dog, bluebird,
frog, and lamb, her broken back legs glued.

I barely remember the child
who collected fragile creatures.
Or even the student who underlined sentences
in a paperback on poetic meter and form
back in the college I recently fled.
Tucked inside are three sheets of poems
by Sylvia Plath. Our professor offered these
in apology for the few women authors in the book.
Plath's poems bristle with nets, needles, and bee stings.
The ends of some lines punch hard as fists.

I slide the paperback onto the shelves my father built.
Stacked college catalogs are bright with beckoning.
No one suggested a girl might be back
in her old bedroom after six weeks.
I flip through a gold-yellow book of myths,
a worn volume with tales of children lost in a forest
and the girl with a red hood stopped by a wolf.

Neighbors say she should have listened to her mother.
No dillydallying, picking flowers,
no talking to strangers, for God's sake.
They whisper that she was naive,
suggest: *That would never happen to me.*

Cold Sky

I open my nail scissors, study my wrists.
No. I pick up my stuffed snowman,
cloth turned by time to the color of old teeth.
His stitched expression is more resigned
than friendly. I touch his eyes,
pluck one black thread, then several more.

Last winter and spring I volunteered
at a hotline in a church basement.
An evening could pass with no calls.
But we were told it mattered
that troubled people knew we were there.
If someone called and mentioned scissors
and skin, would I have just listened
or would I have begged, trying to sound calm,
Please don't kill yourself?

I walk through the kitchen, past the dog
sleeping by the radiator, my mother's back
to me as she peers into the oven.
I put on my blue jacket and boots.
Shallow snow glistens under the moon.
Iced boughs are too heavy to shift in the wind.
Once, a girl with my name straddled branches,
knew their bends, the roughness and pitch of pine.

My boots squeal like small, hurt animals.
I take them off, peel down my socks.
The fire of snow on skin tells me I'm here. Alive.
But the dark sky stays silent and far away.

Jeannine Atkins

The Ouija Board

My mother turns as I come back in the house,
but she doesn't ask what I was doing.
She names a boy who called again.
Your father told him why you're here.
He left the number at his dorm.

College, where most of my friends are supposed to be.
I glance at her note, but instead
call someone I never kissed.
Greg, a high school senior, invites me to his house.
There, I keep my story short as spitting,
ending with, *I'm okay.* Not because it's true,
but because I need the soothing sound of the sentence.

Greg's face shifts, but he keeps his back
straight as Buddha. He's silent, as we were taught
when we both worked at the hotline.
Greg doesn't push me to say more
or signal that I should stop.
He doesn't ask many questions or offer answers.

When I choose to stop talking,
he takes out a Ouija board the color of weak tea.
The board is light but too thick to bend.
It's printed with letters, numerals, and symbols.

We rest our fingertips on the heart-shaped pointer,
hoping it will glide and spell out messages
from beings mostly gone from earth.
Some people feel a breeze, he says.
Some can hear knocking.

I'm uneasy, scared it's me on the other side,
too close to the dead who are asked to speak.
We wait, but our hands don't move.

Greg says, *Sometimes it's like that.*
You have to believe in the unseen.
He puts away the board and suggests
we visit a psychic a friend introduced him to.
He doesn't name the friend, which is his habit
when referring to boys who touch each other
in the dark but glance to the side
when they pass each other in school corridors.

Bad things happened to Lillian, he says.
Maybe in different lifetimes. She might have
something to teach you. She lives in Vermont.

I don't want to go to Vermont.
My voice rises and splits on the last word.

Greg shrugs, suggests instead
next weekend we climb a nearby mountain.
It's one I've climbed before and isn't high.
He looks at my feet with the scowl
he once directed at my long, light hair,
then gave me a lecture on conditioner.
Now he notes that I need real hiking boots.
He instructs me to keep the leather supple
by lathering them with wax or mink oil,
then baking them in a low oven.

Please

Boots and a mountain forge a plan.
Training for the hotline in the church basement,
we learned that even a small promise to a stranger
–we might ask them to call the next day or week–
could help keep someone alive.

Working in pairs, girl and boy, sometimes
Greg and I turned off the buzzing overhead lights.
Small lamps cast a glow on two steel desks
by walls lined with the dark spines
of old hymnals or tomes from theological school.
In the dim, musty air, we thumbed through
the binder where volunteers left notes about calls.

We startled when the phone rang.
I remember the grip of my hand on the receiver
of a phone about the size and heft of a melon.
Mostly I listened, as we were taught,
though we often began by asking, *Where are you?*
to assure safety. We tried to keep callers
on the phone if we sensed danger.
If a girl started a sentence
she might feel she must end it,
or even move into a short story, claiming time.

We were warned that even
the word *hope* can sound preachy.
I never said, *Please don't kill yourself.*
But I remember thinking those words, fiercely.
I wanted someone, anyone, everyone, to keep on.

The Kitchen Radiator

The linoleum on the floor is red with black specks.
The refrigerator, bought on sale,
is the glossy green of hard candy.
Mom and I silently slice bread, drain beans.
When I arrived back home, she told me
she called my grandmothers, aunts,
and sister, who's away at college,
So you don't have to say what happened.
Mom must have passed along a thin version
of what I told policemen, who called my father.
She told me, *Put it behind you.*

I unbox the hiking boots I chose for their red laces.
I smear them with the kind of wax Greg advised,
then set the boots on the radiator, but not in the oven.
There's too much that can go wrong.

Stolen

I call the boy I talked to in high school corridors,
his father's car, the woods, but rarely on the phone.
It's the wrong place to stutter through silences,
but I don't want to navigate touching.
Even over the wires I feel his ache
to fix and I can't stand it. I can't stop it.
He says nothing wrong
but he can't say anything right. Or maybe that's me.

When he says he wants to see me,
I say the drive from his college is too long.
He doesn't protest, as he hadn't last summer
when I paused his hands, wanting to wait
for something closer to love, whatever that is.
He didn't push, gentleness I then took for granted.

I can't be with someone who'd know what I lost
besides virginity, that stupid, medieval word.
A stranger stole my freshman year at college,
my claims to imagination and faith in the future.
Policemen took my plaid dress with the white collar,
shaping it into a short story they could use.
It may be folded or hung in city archives,
untouched, unwanted, but holding evidence:
blood, semen, microscopic clues.

Climbing

Greg parks his mother's car by the road
instead of the main lot by the ski lifts.
He points to a trail that he says
is a little longer, but you see more.
The early snow has melted,
but left fallen leaves the color of mud
under pines, hemlocks, and trees with bare branches.

While walking, Greg brings up his belief
that my kind of meditation, silent chanting
for twenty minutes twice a day, isn't likely
to help me reach transcendence, a word
that rises like a billboard, wrecking the green view.
His approach requires more solitude
and accepting suffering as a major part of life.
We argue about karma, an idea that seems mean.
Why should one wrong act lead to another?

Greg tells me his teacher for senior English
is the young man who taught plays and myths
from Italy and Greece in the world lit class we took.
His hair and mustache were shiny as black licorice.
He wore flat cotton shoes. Greg tells me in senior English
he introduced beatnik writers like Jack Kerouac,
who sought freedom and some kind of holy spirit
speeding across state borders. *What are you reading?*

I remember the copies of poems folded
into our anthology. *Have you heard of Sylvia Plath?*

Didn't she kill herself? He frowns. *Shouldn't*
you be reading something more inspiring?

I don't know much about her life.
Someone mentioned she died young,
but in those early weeks of class, we focused on meter.

We may be more than halfway up the mountain
when Greg asks, *What will you do?*
When I say I hope to go back to the college I left,
he asks, *Isn't it getting kind of late?*

I hadn't kept track of how many classes I'd missed.
But he's probably right. I thought I'd return
to Florida when the police called saying
they had more photographs for me to look at,
but I'd heard nothing from them.

You should think of transferring to UMass,
Greg says. *I might apply there next spring.*
Maybe study Greek or Chinese literature.
Or forestry. I'd like to help the trees.

Or if you're going to write–When did I tell him that?–
you can do that anywhere. Staying open to the divine.

Life might be a school, but is it a good one?
And I have doubts about counting on grace.
We step out from under branches to the summit's
smooth rocks, lichen, and low brush.
The sun is sinking fast, leaving long shadows.

Seasons

We swiftly admire the view, then head
toward a trail that looks like the one we left.
Another path looks almost the same.
As Greg heads to the first trail, I ask,
Are you sure it's the right one?
He says, *At least we'll be going down. Come on.*

Haste seems like a good idea.
I forgot how early dark comes in November.
I didn't bake my boots or break them in.
The skin on the backs of my ankles has split.
My socks are too thin. No one said anything about socks.

I try to stay steady on the slope, which is getting hard to see.
I slip on a rock while crossing a stream.
Cold water spills into my boots.
Isn't evening when bears come out? My throat closes.
I stop from crying by yelling, *This was a stupid idea.*
You picked the wrong path. We shouldn't have come.

Greg turns to look at me.
It's good to see you can get angry.

Standing under bare branches,
I raise my arms as the goddess Demeter

might have, pausing on the edge of earth
that opened. Her daughter fell
or was dragged to the underworld.
When I first read the myth, the word *rape* wasn't used.
Did Demeter advise her daughter
to forget what happened? No.
She fought to get Persephone back,
punished the rapist and the world
that didn't pay enough attention to one girl's grief.
The furious mother split time into seasons,
ripped off green leaves, clenched them
until they crumbled in chilled air.

The Dark Bottom of the Mountain

As Greg and I reach the road, no parked cars are in sight.
If I'd paid more attention to geography,
I'd have realized a mountain small at the top
has a wide base. I say, *The car could be miles away.*

We should hitchhike. We'll probably get a ride
faster if you put out your thumb.
Don't look at me like that. I know it's not right,
but people are more likely to stop for a girl.

No! My judgment has already been in question.
Now I must be cautious forever.
I say, *We're not going to hitchhike.*

Only a few cars pass.
Yellow headlights and red rear lights
blaze and bleed from nowhere.
I unlace my boots and walk on the side
of the road in soaked socks.
My soles hurt, but I can't let my boots
rub the backs of my heels any rawer.
Each step is painful but I keep on,
cradling my boots, which I don't blame.
I still like the red laces.

Letters

I'm in a bedroom with peeling wallpaper
showing other layers of floral prints.
I'm not a beatnik hopping on or off a freight train
or meeting free spirits in Greenwich Village taverns.
But remembering Greg saying people
can write anywhere, I find an old notebook.

In September and the beginning of October,
I was taking two creative writing classes,
though I never said out loud or silently
that I wanted to be a writer.
One professor advised,
Start a poem as if writing a letter to a friend.
She hoped to curb my language
that could bloom into the obscure.
Write to your mother if she seems friendly,
the professor said. *Anyone who cares.*

I write, Dear Sylvia Plath:
Thank you for speaking up about fire and grime.
How did you dare show matches, crows, and bones?
Did anger save or doom you?
You had a life as a wife and mother
and wrote truthfully, too. I need a new map.

South and North

The carton from my old roommate, Lynn,
includes clothes I left and a hard, shriveled
orange I'd admired on her bookcase.
She emptied a small sample bottle of mouthwash
and filled it with a bit of the ocean,
sand, tiny rocks, and broken seashells.

The package is recognition I won't return
to palm trees, red blossoms the size of soup bowls.
Moss draped from trees
between an art gallery and a clinic
where I could get birth control when I was ready.
I'll no longer share a dorm room where Lynn
and I talked about free will and politics with friends.
One soft-spoken guy increasingly turned
to me and asked my opinions.
Lynn told me he kept looking for me
during the two days I was gone from the room,
eyeing her as if she was my kidnapper.

I'd kind of like to see that boy, but I can't go back.
The dining hall is the only place to eat at the small college.
My last time there I didn't look around
for anyone I might know
but found an empty space to set down my tray.

Behind my back girls were talking
about a campaign for more streetlights on campus.
Someone had recently been attacked walking to her room.
Did you hear about the girl who was raped off campus?

I picked up and put down a glass of milk.
If I turned and introduced myself,
the conversation might stop,
as if I were the uninvited guest to the castle.
Fairy godmothers offered christening gifts,
but she bore only prophecy.
Spinning wheels would be burned, needles hidden.
At sixteen the girl was left not dead, not alive.
The whole village froze over.

I walked back to the dormitory.
My roommate told me the story was in newspapers,
but not my name. *They mean to protect your privacy.*
That had been taken. And why did I need
shielding when I did nothing wrong?

I bought a plane ticket back to Massachusetts.
I flew over the beaten-down railroad tracks,
the small church nailing its steeple into sky
by a yard where my back had flattened grasses.

I flew between two parts of the country, two girls.
For a few hours I was thankful
to be nowhere but in sky.

Errand

Mom asks me to pick up some prescriptions
and a carton of cigarettes at the drugstore
where I started working at sixteen.
After school I leapt off the school bus,
changed into an easy-wash uniform,
twisted my long hair to the back of my head,
and took my place
behind the counter to make cherry Cokes
or pour free cups of coffee for policemen.

I learned to recognize Miss Mary Warner.
Without being asked, I scooped vanilla ice cream
into a silver dish set on one of the paper doilies
kept just for her. I was told she was
a descendant of Mary, famous for her little lamb.
Our town's celebrity silently smoothed her long skirt
as she perched on a stool, spread her hands
gracefully as a ballerina over the dish.
A high school dropout pulled drumsticks
from his pockets and beat a tune on the counter.
Some asked him to keep his hands still,
but I didn't know if he could.

Sometimes a siren rang, then another.
At the shriek of a third alarm,

a young man would slide off the stool
and jog to the fire station a few blocks away.
He and another veteran were regulars.
The daily number of military deaths was printed
in a corner of the newspaper below the weather.
A policeman complained when I wore a black
armband in mourning for the dead in Vietnam.
The pharmacist reminded him
this country has free speech.

He's a kind man and my mother a good customer
but I have enough imagination left to understand
I can't come back to scoop ice cream,
warn children not to twirl on the stools,
face a row of people while wondering
who knows how my life changed late one morning.

Once We Were Children

I sleep too much, bake an apple cake, eat too much.
I don't fit in my body and don't want to have one.
I try to focus on tasks like making soup.
Attention to the sizes and smells of vegetable chunks
staves off the dangerous past and unknown future.
But cooking and compliments can form a chain.
I can't become someone who can't leave a stove.

When supper is ready, I go upstairs to wake my brother
in his bedroom where he retreats right after school.
He wears headphones as he naps under
a rough blanket our father brought back from the army.
I call my brother's name loudly, standing beside
shelves with blue jay and turkey feathers,
old painted models of airplanes and monsters.
Long ago he and I oversaw a tiny town
we made from shoeboxes. We cut windows
we framed with scraps of cloth hung on toothpicks.
Our swirling hands made animals the size of acorns
fly from one roofless house to another.

Now I lift the headphones.
Electric guitars and elaborate drumming leak out.
My brother promises to come eat with us.
I don't say how much I miss him when he's gone.

The Library

Across from the war memorial on the town common
a marble statue honors the local lamb said
to have followed Mary to school.
You don't have to have a title like general
or president to deserve a memorial.
A farm animal can be remembered,
or an ordinary schoolgirl like those I used to read about,
sweeping floors or sewing,
before they became who they were meant to be.

In the library, two women break their conversation,
greet me, but don't ask what I'm doing here.
I guess they've heard why I came back home.
I step around a table of magazines and bestsellers.
In a narrow aisle between back shelves, I find the book
about Hester Prynne, who stitched her own red letter,
kept secrets, and raised a child alone.
Tess of the d'Urbervilles tended chickens and cows,
gave birth as a teenager, walked to the gallows.
In eleventh grade we discussed whether the tragic flaw
was human character or growing industry.
We were supposed to admire the girls' lack of complaint,
call their silence dignity. Like Joan of Arc,
keeping her head high as men set her on fire.

I head to the card catalog, silently sing part
of the alphabet song before the box labeled with a *P*.
I shuffle through index cards, find no books
by Plath, Sylvia. I shut the small drawer,
making a soft thud like that of an oven door.

Saved

Outside the library, I see Diane's mother, her arms full
of romances and what my mother calls gossip magazines.
She tells me her daughter is training to work
in a dental office, living
with the guy she dated in high school.
Diane and I drifted apart after she became a cheerleader
and took courses in what was called the business track,
with typing, shorthand, English classes with no novels
or poems, accounting courses instead of geometry.

But when I was seven and my mother
was in the hospital, I lived in their small house.
We ate in the kitchen, where Diane's mother
served food straight from pots or pans.
If someone didn't like what was in them,
we weren't made to stare at a plate.
She simply made a peanut butter sandwich.
It was a beautiful choice: jam or not. I'm still grateful.

Now I call Diane. I don't know where to begin
an account of why I came back,
and I'm waiting for an ending.
I don't expect something grand like in Shakespeare.
Not comedy or tragedy, but maybe a breath of justice.
I start with a summary of the middle,

say I'm okay, though that's a place I visit.
It's not a steady home.

Diane says I'm brave. The word separates us,
like a cloak meant to hide a naive girl
who walked in the wrong place at the wrong time.
Can you be brave if you have no choice?
Back when Diane and I were friends,
she was the bold one, leading me
past *No Trespassing* signs
into abandoned barns and meadows.
When we played truth or dare, she chose the latter.
One afternoon we climbed the hill to her house
when a car stopped beside us.
A man leaned over the passenger seat,
rolled down the window, asked, *Want a ride?*

Diane started to open the car door.
I pulled her away, shook my head at the man,
who shrugged and drove on even as Diane
cried out in protest. I cut through her words.
She wouldn't talk to me as we walked the rest of the way.
She could be reckless, blowing bubbles in her milk
against the cafeteria rules, or careless,
letting gum wrappers fall to the road.

I was sorry she was mad at me,
but at least we weren't locked in a car,
facing a fate too terrible for anyone to tell
but that might end as a body in a ditch.

At her house a car was in the driveway,
though her father would be at work.
In the kitchen, I recognized the driver
leaning against the refrigerator drinking lemonade.
Have you met Diane's uncle? my friend's mother asked.
She laughed as Diane told what happened
and said, *I told her I knew him!* Did she?
Diane continued to sulk, but I didn't care.
I'd looked out for us. That wasn't wrong.

Under the Slanting Ceiling

A flimsy ballerina in a jewelry box no longer turns.
I should clean my room, but it's hard to know what to save.
Once, my high school notebooks seemed to hold
scraps of wisdom, but I can't find much now
besides a line about the pasteboard mask in *Moby Dick*.
I shuffle old papers, moving backward
instead of forward, though I applied to UMass.
Now there's something else to wait for.

In Honors English we were taught to take in stride
horrors on the page, allowed a sigh or eye roll
but no screams or tears even as Oedipus
married his mother, then gouged out his eyes.
Like in biology class, we're coached
to look casual about death.

Some girls complained that everything
we read was depressing. I saw their point,
but didn't want to be called sentimental.
The clever boys drew strict lines between
who was smart and stupid, cynical and hopeful.

I was already the vegetarian who refused to dissect a frog.
The biology teacher said, *Fine, you can watch.*
He probably figured out I wouldn't be a scientist.

He tolerated my lab partner's absences
and weeping over her boyfriend missing in Vietnam.
After she returned to class, I tried to catch her up
on assignments, but whatever I said
seemed to be letting her down.

What's Left Out

Maybe there's no reason to throw away
a jewelry box with only one broken part.
But I don't save my notebooks, rip apart pages
with entries about Richard Wright's *Native Son*.
The teacher and the smart boys
discussed our unjust society.
Could it drive a Black man to murder a White woman?
The protagonist held a pillow over her mouth.
He smashed in the head of a young Black woman.
A pillow. A brick. Breath ending.
I didn't say the novel turned my stomach.
I didn't want to look ignorant of literature and history,
asking why we don't know more
about the murdered young women, Mary and Bessie?

I kept quiet rather than risk saying something wrong.
The days of being told that
everyone is alike inside were gone.
When I was six, I saw a news photograph
of a girl my age walking into a Louisiana school
where she was the first Black student.
Ruby Bridges kept her face calm.
Her hair ribbons were crisp and her socks stayed up.
If Ruby came to join our class in Massachusetts,
wouldn't we say, *Come play horses with us?*

Surely we would have pushed back our desks,
scraping, bumping to make room for one more.

No longer six years old, but sixteen, was Ruby,
like me, baffled by *Native Son* and *Moby Dick*?
Was she making plans to go away to college?
Did anyone offer to help or ask what it had been like
to pass people throwing eggs and rocks, shoving,
pushing, pointing, screaming vile words?
Did anyone recently ask, *Dear Ruby:*
Do you scream in your nightmares?
Do you want to be a writer? What are your dreams?

Blades

I take out a black-speckled notebook.
My hair feels brittle as toast.
I want to be a bowl, or soft as bread,
but I am a steel needle, a thorn.

No, say it straight and plain, but how?
My poetry professor warned us to be leery
of the thesaurus. Did I really need: *violet*,
beautiful, all the syllables in *extraordinary*?
Rather than lift spells of fairies,
find the tools of carpenters, farmers, and cooks:
nails, shovels, or spoons.
Mud can be as good as shine. Try to smell it.

I wait for an idea. Instead,
memory steps up, waving a knife.

A Chance

I twist the spiraling cord tethering the phone
as an admissions worker tells me that once someone
attends another college, she can't just start over.
Though I was accepted to UMass last spring,
I now need two years of college
to apply as a transfer student.
Rules are rules, though I wonder if she's mad
that the university wasn't my first choice.

Now that I'm told I'm not welcome, I really want to go.
I remember my high school guidance counselor
saying: *My door is always open.*
Or maybe that was another counselor, on television.
I drive to the high school and enter
without books, as if this is a first day.
I tell the guidance counselor why I left college.
The three words feel like spitting glass from my mouth,
short, so we can move on.

The counselor leans back, but his face doesn't crumple.
He takes a breath, rocks forward, murmurs something kind.
I'll call someone at UMass. See what can be done.

It's not a promise, but the relief makes me bold
enough to take a small unplanned journey up the stairs.

I glance in the classroom where I once recited
a poem I memorized by W. B. Yeats:
Turning and turning in the widening gyre
. . . Things fall apart; the centre cannot hold.

The teacher I now see through the glass
on the door liked me, though she never gave
me the encouraging or exasperated looks
she bestowed on boys who showed promise as writers.
Once, she propped a print of a Bruegel painting
on the blackboard's chalk tray. It was busy with details
of peasants, fishermen, sheep, and a dog.
She wrote the word *ekphrastic* on the board,
talking about poems in conversation with art.

Only as Mrs. Johnson read W. H. Auden's poem
did we turn our gazes from beings on land or sea
to the painted sky where a boy fell,
feathers and waxen wings on fire.
No one looked up. Everyone was busy.

Unsentimental

Before I chose the poem about the turning gyre,
I thumbed through a poetry anthology
stopping at one by Gerard Manley Hopkins:
Márgarét, áre you gríeving
Over Goldengrove unleaving?

I liked it, but was afraid boys might mock
the sad girl, the shine. "Spring and Fall"
looked dangerously close to sentimental
with its leaves, sigh, and heart. We were taught
to be cautious of words like *grandmother*,
the moon, *birds* or anything with wings,
flowers, unless there was plenty of dirt.

But *sentimental* can be an adjective waved
to keep half the population out of halls of greatness.
Boys ridicule *Little Women* without reading the novel
with a mother who says she's angry every day of her life.
Love doesn't come easy. Jo March's fury
could be quiet, but wearing an ink-stained smock,
she kicked a way into the garret.

Pessimism isn't trickier than optimism.
Spotting a bad ending coming isn't proof
of intelligence. I was afraid of the wrong things.

Absences

I whisk vinegar and oil, salt and pepper,
in a wooden bowl, add lettuce and tomatoes
the way my grand-mère did, tossing the salad at the table.
My father's praise of the lasagna I made
echoes across the too-bare table.
My brother is somewhere, Mom in her bedroom,
where she spends most of her time since I got home.

When I left for college I thought that might change.
Mom was in hospitals through a lot of my childhood,
when my brother, sister, and I stayed with other families.
But she rallied shortly before I started high school.
She curled her hair with bobby pins, ironed skirts,
put on lipstick, and a few evenings a week
drove to a state college in the nearest city.
She underlined sentences
in a history book the color of clover.
She lent me her old copy of *Gone with the Wind*
but told me that many plantation owners
were crueler than Scarlett's family.
I'd been taught that bighearted soldiers from the North
freed the enslaved and kept the states united.
Mom said that wasn't the end of the story.

She graduated college just before I left for one.
But it turned out few high schools

were looking for a history teacher.
Maybe she's still looking for work, but I mostly see
her watching television or organizing pills
in a toolbox with three pullout tiers.
My brother tells me he's sampled some:
None make you feel very good.

Whole Wheat Bread

Just before Christmas my sister drives across
the country with friends on their way to Boston.
She's two years older than me,
known in the family as the smart one.
In elementary school, boys called her stuck-up
for raising her hand with right answers.
In eighth grade she won a regional spelling bee.
A photo was printed in the newspaper, a trophy
held between her and the second-place winner.
The tall boy raised the trophy so she had to stretch,
looking like she was grasping for what was hers.
Our mother shook her head in disgust, lit a cigarette.

Now my sister tells me about getting up before daybreak,
working at a co-op bakery
making pale brown loaves of bread.
She teaches me how to mix and knead dough,
how to tell it's ready to rise
when it feels smooth as an earlobe.

The Unfinished Quilt

An apartment on our third floor is rented
by a couple from Texas. People admire
the art teacher who our family got to call Ruth.
She taught us to draw birds and bowls,
told us about perspective and that making mistakes
is as good as coloring within lines.

One Saturday afternoon Ruth comes down
and says her husband is busy
this snowy weekend maintaining ski slopes.
And Alan doesn't think it's supper unless there's red meat.
She asks me to come up as she tries a new recipe.
A quilt stands on an oval frame,
made with cloth in various shades of red
cut to the sizes of stamps or sticks of gum.
A painting with blue and black splashes and slashes
dries on an easel by the window.
Some neighbors gave Alan slack for being a veteran,
but before he began work on ski lifts at the mountain,
others regularly asked me if he had a job yet.
When I said that he painted, they asked if he sold any.

Ruth broils eggplant, sprinkles cinnamon
into tomato sauce while I thumb through
their magazines, stop at a poem that stuns me.

The columns of words are split by the stapled spine,
stanzas opening like two wings.

After we eat the moussaka, I stand by Ruth
at the sink, talking about how I'll start at UMass soon.
Passing me a plate to dry, she says, *I'm glad you're okay.*
The last word is one my mother might have given her.
Alan said he'd like to kill him. Ruth shakes her head.
I told him: What good would that do?

True, death would change little.
Still, something bristles inside me, waking, alive.
It isn't murder or gallantry I want,
but the gift that there are more ways to end my story.
My gaze turns from the plate in my hand
to the abstract painting on the easel,
the quilt frame holding crimson cotton patches,
purple and red silk shining like jewels.

PART II

Safety Pins and Shears

New Walls

I rip Anne Sexton's poem "The Ambition Bird"
from Ruth and Alan's magazine. I pack the two pages
in a knapsack I haul into a seven-story dormitory
with a pastoral name. My father stands behind
me as I get a key from a smiling young woman
who says she's an RA. When I look puzzled,
she explains, *Resident Assistant.* I'm still confused.
Maybe I shouldn't have skipped orientation.

In my new room, textbooks are stacked
at one end of a counter.
A telephone squats like a fat frog in the middle.
The walls are the pale blue of pills.
My roommate's bedspread has tufts and fringe,
a stuffed bear propped on the pillow.
Angela has a soft body and serious face.
Her clothes are as plain as the cover
of the Bible by her bed. She says she majors
in nursing and asks me where I'm from.
In my last college we answered
that question by naming states.
At UMass people mostly mention towns or cities.

I ask my father to help me drag the bed frame
to the hallway for a custodian to store.

I can tell he thinks a mattress on the floor
is a bad idea, but like me, he hates to argue.
I put my clothes in drawers, use them to hide
the dried orange and bottled sea my old roommate sent.
I don't want questions about where I've been.
But I tape the poem to the cinder-block wall.
All night dark wings / flopping in my heart.

The Long Hall

In the dorm's bathroom or hallway, I greet girls
who wear nightgowns printed with birds or hearts.
Some ask, *Why are you starting college now?*
They mean not in fall, like normal people.
I try to create an interesting story instead of a sad one.
I observe corners of eyes or mouths, but find no chance
to offer a word that can wreck a conversation.

I call my mother and tell her I'm doing okay.
Lots of people skip a lot of classes,
sleep too much, don't they? Hate the dining halls.
Buy a pint of ice cream to eat in semisecret.

Stumbling

I take notes about clouds, thunder, and hurricanes
in the back of an auditorium, earning a science credit.
I do little French homework, counting on
going to class to keep up, though
that strategy didn't work well in high school.
I take a survey course where novels were chosen
because they were supposed to matter,
but we spend class combing paragraphs
for wrong words, mocking characters,
condemning coincidences.

I miss reading the way I did as a child,
finding refuge in a log cabin, tepee, fire escape,
or a house with four sisters: Jo carried pen and ink
to the garret, Amy drew on the walls.
I miss stumbling into moments
when a girl in a book seemed to become me.

The Elevator

Overhead lights flicker. They're not meant to stay on
over aisles between the library bookshelves.
I can't find poetry books or fiction, so speak
to a woman behind a desk. She tells me many books
are in storage while a new library is being built.
You can fill out a card to request them.

I don't have titles in mind. Even if I did,
I may not need what I ask for, but a book
on the shelf below it or another within reach.
I go back downstairs, find a chair,
untie my boots' red laces, take out
a notebook soft and brown as old leaves.

I bear myself still as judgment
while a forest grows inside me, a storm.
Is that too much metaphor? What if it's not metaphor?
My backward glance goes too far,
snagging a girl I don't want to be.
Memory snarls my hair, bullies a way into my body,
tears calendars, pushes me back to October.

Behind my back, the elevator trills and dings.
Metal doors clap open and shut.
My back straightens, an icicle. Who's here?
No one. Anyone.

Small Rooms

I walk through cold rain to a used bookshop in town,
buy a finger-thin book called *Ariel*.
I read the introduction about
how Sylvia Plath's life and writing merged.
Her poems offer bees, needles, hair on fire.
A tulip can be a weapon.
Teeth marks seem to pierce pages.
She rolls, rips, and squeezes words shut,
to be unbuttoned in a reader's own fashion.
With blade-sharp words,
she fixed cruelty and love to one page.

What I think can't be said
can
be said.
Can her poems become rooms to write in?

The Circle

Angela asks me to chip in for a necklace
for the resident assistant's birthday.
Apparently I'm expected to show up for cake, too.
I stand behind girls crowding into her room.
The RA opens the box, shrieks
as if the necklace is made of real diamonds.
Girls shout, *Happy Birthday*, elbow a way toward her.
A few look close to tears, which seems over the top.
As they take turns flinging their arms around her,
the RA looks over the pressed-together girls at me.
Is she mad this is the first time I've come to her room?
Something cracks inside me. My eyes feel wet.
The necklace looks tacky, but is that so wrong?

Not an Ending

Back in our room, I tell Angela why I left
my first college. She rushes to consolation,
offers words meant to smooth wrinkles in my story.
She asks for a few details, her eyes shifting
as if hoping facts will show what happened to me
is unlikely to happen to her.
I would have … You should have …
Invisible pebbles cast into wind tap-tap on nothing.
She wouldn't have been there or walked alone.
She'd have worn something else,
fought longer and harder, yelled louder.

When she asks, *Are you okay now?*
I say, *Yes,* because that's the answer
she hopes will stop
this story from spreading. And I don't want
to be someone who says she's not all right.

Warnings

I practice clutching a key so it might be used as a weapon.
Girls are taught safety rules that are thin as pins.
We're cautioned to avoid night,
though I was grabbed on a bright morning.
Be careful where you go. Don't stay stuck at home.
Not all guys are bad. Watch out.
Don't walk alone. I'm always alone,
assessing shades of danger
that might skulk or leap from newspapers,
books, a voice overheard in a cafeteria.

Don't change your life because of this. Change your life.
I can avoid a show, a song, places, people,
but memory is an acrobat, has its own tricks,
coming from almost anywhere to trip me.
I'm only heading back from class
like any girl, busy with dreams,
when a man stops his car, asks, *Want a ride?*
I hurry off but can't escape a sick bird hiding
inside me, beating ragged, mostly useless wings.

American History

I finish the semester badly and head home.
I sit by my parents' bedroom window
with its view of the grocery store, hardware store,
the pizza shop that sells donuts on Sunday mornings.
My mother rarely reminisces, but she's told me
that when she was my age she worked in an office.
I don't know what she did besides type,
but she was sad when the job ended.
No one told her that millions of women
were dismissed at the end of World War II
when jobs were rearranged for returning soldiers.
She was happy to marry one of them,
but she hated the house he chose far from a suburb
where she could take a train to New York.

Some in our town seem to measure goodness
by how long one's ancestors lived here.
My mother always felt under suspicion.
When I was young, she used a mix
to bake brownies for a church bake sale.
They were returned by a woman who said
they wouldn't sell desserts that weren't homemade.

After that, Mom seldom sat in the sanctuary,
but taught Sunday school for a while.

She wrote a children's play that was never
performed, which might be for a dozen reasons.
She saved the skit in her bottom bureau drawer
but never wrote another.

Mom stayed home, reading magazines
nurses left and books about Puritan times.
She told me men held trials where women
called witches were dunked underwater.
Those who quietly sank might be innocent,
not wicked or crazy. If a woman resisted,
splashed, sputtered, fought her way up,
she was bound and sent to a scaffold.

Rocks and Sand

I find a summer job as a mother's helper
in a neighborhood of big houses with tidy lawns.
Many children are minded by college girls
sort of like me, our hair loose or in ponytails,
wearing jeans and untucked shirts, ready for business.
The mom who hired me probably married
when the Kennedys were in the White House.
She wears her hair puffed, pulled, and sprayed like Jackie's,
looks poised on her way to and from a tennis club.

I chat with the two older boys
as I make them sandwiches.
They may wander as they like.
The six-year-old sometimes
comes home from forays in tears.
The nine-year-old befriends neighbors' dogs.
He pines for one of his own, or a gorilla.
Mostly I take the toddler on neighborhood walks.
She picks up rocks, meets friends in sandboxes.
They dig holes, roll toy trucks, build castles,
towers, and tunnels that crash, then start again.

I turn as a girl shrieks, flaps her arms
by bees in nearby pink-and-white clover.
As she runs home, I assure the child I care for:

Bees are looking for flowers, not people.
If you don't hurt them, they won't hurt you.
Who told me that? Likely not my mother,
but a neighbor, a teacher,
someone stepping in as one, like me.

The Broken Candy House

Not family, but not called the help, I'm content
to eat cheese sandwiches or cups of yogurt
in the kitchen with the little girl but dislike
being exiled from the dining room, always.
In the basement where the children play when it rains
are stacked landscapes and portraits their mom
painted in college. I wouldn't say they aren't good,
but she said that herself. And *Art can be a nice way to relax.*

Art must be more. One can't just stop and stick efforts
in the basement. But I'm not here to offer opinions.
I keep thoughts to myself, like Jane Eyre,
a governess who was poor and plain
yet proud enough to narrate a thick book about love.

I have a bedroom over the garage with curtains
with flounces and matching bedspread.
At night I'm too tired to write
after emptying sand from my sneakers,
after the little girl says, *Again,*
over the book with the cheerful cover
of a house studded with gumdrops and peppermints
that a girl and boy can't resist tasting.
A tale that turns on a push, an oven, and a scream.

Fall

My assigned roommate in the high-rise dormitory
arrived early for cheerleading practice. Her things flood
the room, clothes strewn across the bed meant for me.
In hers, hair sprawls from under a blanket
hastily thrown to cover two pairs of knees and elbows.
We try to work out a system so she can have
privacy with her boyfriend, but it fails.
I hate the dormitory elevator, where hands
slide into pockets, slip out cash or small bags.
The stairwell where I pass nine shut doors isn't better.

A friend from high school lives on the nineteenth floor.
We used to share oranges
sitting on the floor outside the cafeteria.
She wrote me notes, adorning their backs with stars
whose sides stretched into the sides of another.
But I never liked her boyfriend,
who flirted with me and other girls.

His dark clothes are now spread over the bed
by record albums I don't think she'd choose.
Her laughter is unnaturally high though nothing is funny.
She stares out the window looking toward blue hills
or the dangerous air between the glass and ground.
She tells me the windows don't open.
I nod. I knew that. I don't go back.

The Basement Room

Changing dorm rooms is against the rules, but so
is the boyfriend who isn't a student and refuses to leave.
My old friend Greg, who moved into a suite
on another floor here, helps me carry my things
to a smaller dormitory named after a transcendentalist.
There, a tall girl with short brown hair stands formally
or maybe stonily. I would have been annoyed, too,
if my hope for a private room was disrupted.

I try to stay unobtrusive, which Susan appreciates
as well as the poem about the ambition bird
I tape across from her wall with old playbills, postcards
of gargoyles and curious figures in stained glass.
Susan, do not call her Sue, double majors in French,
which she plans to teach in high school,
and theater, where she finds most of her friends.
She likes Greg, though disapproves of meditation:
Why would anyone want to be peaceful? The world is a mess.

A History of Art

I register for courses in Shakespeare, French, math,
Bible as Literature, and a survey of art history.
In a dark auditorium blinking with slides,
the professor tells us he moved from California
to be closer to Paul Gauguin's panel in Boston's
Museum of Fine Arts: *Where Do We Come From?*
What Are We? Where Are We Going?

In following classes, the professor mostly
sticks to the chronology in our hefty book.
I skip ahead to Pablo Picasso's broken and patched people,
then back to the Impressionists. I love Claude Monet's
ponds, water lilies, bridges, and reflections.
His lines are more blurred than
those in the oil paintings my grand-mère made
back before she had my father and his brothers.
One hangs in our dining room, framed but without glass.
I used to climb on a radiator to touch its gritty surface.

Traps

In a small house on the edge of campus,
about twenty meditators not drawn to danger,
who've been cautioned not to drink or do drugs,
cross our legs, close our eyes, and tend to silent mantras.
After twenty minutes, we unravel ourselves
and talk over cups of herbal tea. We put on jackets
and wide-toed shoes we left by the door.

Afterward on some Sunday afternoons,
Rachel and I study together while
she waits for the bus that crosses the river
to Northampton, where she goes to Smith College.
In a coffee shop, she admires late afternoon
shadows slanting from glass saltshakers.
She's a year or two ahead of me.
Her art history survey course uses the same text
as my UMass class, with hundreds of pages
about what are supposed to be the best paintings
and sculptures ever, though just two artists are women.

Rachel takes out flash cards she made
by photocopying work from the book,
cutting and pasting these on thin cardboard,
and writing names of artists and dates on the backs.
I haven't used flash cards since fifth grade,

but I like trying to distinguish Madonnas,
then mispronouncing German and Italian names.

Taking breaks from the Renaissance, we talk
about which meditators we think are cute.
She confides her dream to paint her own pictures.
I tell her I kind of want to write.
You can, Rachel says, then flips forward
in *The History of Art.* I tell her I like Monet.

The world isn't that pink, Rachel says.
Her hair is a color between smoke and sand,
spiraling and lifting from her neck.
She turns to self-portraits of a man
in a battered straw hat, another with a bandaged ear.
She says, *I kind of wish I loved someone less popular*
than Van Gogh, though he wasn't when he was alive.
It was his brother who told him to carry on.

Sometimes you need just one person to believe.

Vincent van Gogh was mentally ill. He didn't kill
himself just because he never sold a painting.

I look at a painted vase of vividly purple iris.

The edges of petals look sharp. Dangerous.
Like flowers in Sylvia Plath's poems.

Oh, do you know her? Rachel asks.
The girls in my dorm are passing around
her novel. She died almost ten years ago,
but The Bell Jar *just came out in America.*

What's a bell jar?

Clear jars we used in my intro to botany
course to grow tropical plants.
The glass traps heat and humidity to keep them alive.
I guess the trap part was her metaphor.
She writes that she hates her mother.
Rachel looks small, like a person turning into a portrait.
My mother died when I was eight.

Rachel, I'm sorry.

My mom was beautiful. She set the dinner table
with candles, though we didn't light them, she says.
When I was in first grade, she used to safety pin
notes to my cardigans for the teacher.
When I was sick, she'd sit with her hand on my forehead.
I thought she sat like that all night, but she probably left.

Rachel sweeps the flash cards into her backpack.

She pulls out and hands me a copy of *The Bell Jar*.

The book's narrator isn't Sylvia, but no one

can tell them apart. They both interned

in New York at a women's fashion magazine, returned home

to Massachusetts, swallowed a lot of pills,

and spent fall in an asylum instead of college.

The girls told me the ending. Keep it as long as you want.

Half-Hidden

I tuck the novel at the bottom of a stack of books
I'm behind in reading. I open a Bible
edited for lit classes, thick with annotations.
We worked our way through the lines drawn
in Genesis: light breaking from darkness,
dividing land from sea,
animals from people,
who are split into male and female.
Eve eats an apple and everyone
gets lined up to be favored or cast out.

Some stories are familiar from Sunday school.
By shoeboxes of broken crayons, red-handled scissors,
and cotton balls for sheep or clouds, we drew rainbows.
If we wondered about those who didn't fit
on Noah's ark, our questions were hushed.

We brought offering envelopes
with a perforated line down the middle.
One side held money for the church.
The other was meant for the needy beyond.
The church looked all right, with sturdy tables,
plenty of paper, graham crackers, and apple juice.
Given two nickels, I put both in the side of beyond.

We took turns bringing in small things to show others.
When I shook a snow globe, white flakes drifted
over a forest where a girl in a red hood faced a wolf.
A boy grabbed my treasure,
raised and opened his hand.

The clear plastic dome cracked.
Damp flakes and water sloshed over the table.
The teacher leapt up for paper towels,
scolded the boy
while children gasped and patted my back.
I didn't say that I understood the urge to break,
liked seeing jagged edges,
the machinery behind wonder,
the slop and shine of what was not snow.

What Was Missing

The Bell Jar starts near the end of a summer
internship at a New York fashion magazine.
In the novel, a nineteen-year-old based on Sylvia
already feels friendless, reckless,
before heading to a party outside the city.
As I read I beg: *Don't go!* Of course I stop nothing.

Dear Sylvia: The morning after the party
you took a train back to Massachusetts.
When your mother picked you up at the train station,
she asked, *What happened to your face?*

Cut myself is your first lie,
to stop other questions:
How did you meet that man?
Was he drinking? Were you?
When you touched the diamond pin holding his tie,
he plucked it out and handed it to you.
As you dropped it into your beaded purse,
didn't you think he'd expect something back?
He asked you to dance the tango.
When you said you didn't know how,
he said, *Pretend you are drowning.*
Why didn't you run?
Why didn't you stay home?

He led you out to the country club garden,

ripped off your purse,

then the top half of your gown.

The ground slammed up.

Slut, the man yelled, shaping the story

so that whatever happens now a girl is to blame.

You aimed your high heels at his legs,

made a fist you slammed into his nose.

He touched the blood,

ran his wet fingertips down your face.

Fortunately, you wrote

—we all memorize that transitional word—

the band had stopped playing, people were leaving.

You knocked on car windows

until you found someone driving back

to the city who had room

for a girl with a cape

wrapped over what was missing

of a dress.

Windows

Dear Sylvia: I wish I could save you.
But I can only try to see you
back in the New York hotel, opening
a window. You tossed out gifts
of frothy dresses, cruel underwear.
But left the blood on your face
you kept stiff so it wouldn't crack
on the train or in your mother's gray car.
She handed you a letter she'd opened.
Your story was not good enough for you
to get into a summer writing class at Harvard.

You pretended it didn't matter.
So did your mother, who offered a new plan
teaching you shorthand, that language
girls learned to take notes from powerful men.
As if becoming a secretary might save you.

What if she knew that *last night*
you walked between cars, one hand clutching
a cape over your bare shoulders,
knocking on windows?
Some drivers kept theirs rolled up,
maybe remembered seeing you
touch the jewel that pinned his tie,

then stash it away.
Slut. Whore. Trouble.
Some might have claimed to be heading another way.
Nobody asked, *What's wrong?*

Bruised, bleeding, we knock
and knock on windows, peer in.
Our knuckles hurt. Who can see
girls pleading for a way home?
Car lights flicker and disappear.

Silver Teapots

Rachel and I meet in a small Northampton café.
As I sip my first cup of mocha java coffee,
she confides her crush on a cute, short,
well-spoken boy at the meditation center.
This boy is too calm and certain for me,
though I also don't like guys on the edge.

Rachel talks about having afternoon tea
with antique pots and china cups
in the dormitories Smith students call houses.
The ritual began when studious young ladies
wore floor-length dresses, wide hats, and white gloves.
The lemon bars are good, Rachel says.

I imagine Sylvia wearing a wide skirt and thin sweater,
taking a single, disciplined bite. She sat among girls
watching who took more, measuring hunger.
Sylvia must have crossed the campus carrying books
she read all the way through. She probably understood
the symbols in *Moby Dick* without being told.
Did she already collect burnt matches, needles,
bruised tulips, beehives the shape of old-time ovens?
Was her red bandeau holding back
butter-smooth hair a disguise?

Rachel and I finish our coffee, climb the hill,
pass iron gates. She stops to point out the dormitory

where Sylvia wept over the World of Atoms,
blaming physics class for her depression.
She left this dorm for her internship in New York,
then came back to the house where her mother
dragged an old chalkboard from the cellar.
She set it up in the dining room, circling
her arm as she made a stenographer's curlicues.
White dust smeared her hands.

Sylvia looked out the dining room window, hating
the squeaky wheels of a baby carriage a neighbor pushed.
For days Sylvia couldn't sleep or read or write.
She drew a razor over her skin, making thin red lines.
When her mother left the house,
Sylvia broke the lock on a green metal box,
filled a glass of water she carried to the cellar.
Past the oil burner and spider webs,
she counted forty pills meant for sleep,
swallowed, sank
into the wrinkles of her black coat.

When her mother returned and realized
Sylvia was missing, she searched the house.
She called friends, neighbors, police, and Boy Scouts
who tramped though the neighborhood
and woods in the rain rain rain.
The basement had already been searched,

more sandwiches prepared,

though no one was hungry,

when Sylvia's brother ran back down.

He pushed past the woodpile

where for three days Sylvia lay in old pee and vomit.

She spent months in an asylum.

When she came out, her mother said,

Pretend that what happened was a dream.

Hiding a sense the bell jar could descend again,

Sylvia went back to college where girls

were coached not to bother or pry.

Promise Me

Rachel and I walk toward a brick building
with peaked roofs and tall, narrow windows.
This was where Sylvia lived during her last year here,
Rachel says. *With other scholarship students.*
Sylvia set down plates, carried away
empty cups and knives,
made sure there were no crumbs in the jam.
Then she climbed the stairs to her room
where she sat before her typewriter,
rounded on top like a woodchuck,
a small wild animal, and about its size.
She rolled in a sheet of pale pink paper.

Rachel keeps her gaze fixed to the brick walls
as she says, *It was pills for my mother, too.*
Her voice is low. *She took enough.*

I reach for Rachel's hand.
In our stolid wide-toed shoes we tip
toward what's invisible, beautiful,
or terrible behind those dark windows.
Who found the dead woman? Who cleaned up?

I read that if a parent kills herself,
it's likelier their child might, too, Rachel says.

People say a lot of stupid things.

I don't want to let go of her hand.

It's not a prophecy! You won't, will you?

The Shrunken Orange

Now that I've finished reading *The Bell Jar*,
I should focus on homework. Instead,
as my roommate works late at the campus theater,
I rummage through a box of papers,
the shriveled orange my old roommate sent me,
the bottle holding a bit of foggy water.
Lynn's letters are about a year old,
mostly sent soon after I left Florida.
In one she mentioned that the college stopped
the program I was in that Saturday.
I shut the box but set the old orange on my desk.

I don't want to be alone. I walk to the dorm
where Greg shares a suite with three other guys.
I'm glad no one else is here. I don't care
to hear their strong opinions
on German philosophers, black teas,
Virginia Woolf's profile, and plaid flannel shirts.
Greg lifts a record between his palms,
places it over the turntable. He carefully sets
a needle on the circular line marking "Little Green."

I'm going to Vermont this weekend to see the psychic.
Lillian says to pay attention to little things.
Greg brushes back a lock of hair,

slightly duller than his gold-rimmed glasses.
An almond or pine cone can be a teacher. Want to come?

I don't believe someone can tell my future.

Maybe there isn't a future. People in ancient Egypt
thought time doesn't move forward,
but circles, like the rising and setting sun.
He shows me a page torn from a magazine
about the discovery of murals from an excavated tomb.
A picture is of two men tenderly touching.

The archaeologist says they were both servants
to the king. And buried in the same tomb,
probably brothers. Greg shakes his head.
Have you ever seen brothers
gaze into each other's eyes like that?
I want to try to contact them.

He moves the teacups and sets down a Ouija board.
It's the color of acorns ripe enough to fall,
but not on the ground long enough to darken.
We sit on the floor, let our fingertips hover.
Greg says, *You can invite someone who's gone.*

Leaning in, our hands are light.
If someone is listening on the other side,
they might be more likely to visit an acorn
or oak tree with its rough bark and shifting shade.
Still, I ask Sylvia to leave. I ask her to haunt me.

After Thanksgiving

I study sitting across from my roommate.
Susan's short bob might be in imitation of Joan of Arc.
We went to see an old film based on her life.
Susan likes the heft of right and wrong in Greek plays,
the definitive ends in justice, vengeance, or death.
And French existentialists, plays by Ionesco.
I tell her we read *Rhinoceros* in senior English.
Yikes, those crazy animals coming one after another.
Instead of writing a paper, I baked rhinoceros-shaped
cookies, enough for each person in our class.

Susan laughs. *Did you get a grade?*

I was already accepted to college. It didn't matter.
I packed the cookies close in a box
so the horns wouldn't snap off on the school bus.
At least it was a break from books where women
were punished for wanting even small things.
Hester Prynne stuck forever with that scarlet letter.
And Tess of the d'Urbervilles yearning
for a bit of attention, so was doomed.
Of course she may have been too free with a knife.

The liar and cheat raped her, Susan says.
He deserved what he got.

I take a breath, remember the class discussion
of whether what happened off the page
was likelier to be seduction or a crime.
Some boys said Tess shouldn't have let
herself be fooled by a scoundrel.
She shouldn't have been in the woods,
shouldn't have smiled, shouldn't have fallen asleep.

Now I tell Susan what can be spoken only
to certain people in certain places at certain times.
It's hard to put the story out there
and hard to keep it in.
I'm hundreds of miles away from the man
who said, *Don't tell,* but he lives in me, too.

I'm sorry, Susan says. *That's horrible.*
Did they find him? Is he in jail?

Not yet. I think the police are still looking.
I remember trying to focus on the small black-
and-white photographs policemen shuffled through.
A face is not as still as paper or a frame.

A lot of cases never go to trial. Or it takes a while,

Susan says. *But it seems strange*
they haven't contacted you after a year.
Or maybe nothing is strange. Or everything.

Rape taught me anything can happen.
Still, I clutched the edges of the story
that newspapers and television led me to expect:
Police would catch and put the rapist in jail,
which I then thought of as a place of reform,
and all girls would be safer.

Maybe that won't happen, but I want an ending.
Stories shouldn't stop on nothing, with people
just going on like one rhinoceros after another.
Rhinoceros, rhinoceros, rhinoceros. I hated that play.

Snow

In January I sign up for an American lit survey,
another science requirement. Lured by a small class,
I take an honors seminar on French revolutions.
Ballet I fulfills a PE credit. We repeat pliés
and leg lifts, arrange our backbones, point our toes,
slide them in arcs, gliding to taped piano music.

But snowstorms keep me from classes.
And a yellow caution light that seems
to blink through my belly and breath.
Shadows make me bolt from the dining hall,
buy packaged coffee cake to eat alone.
In classes I look from the professor to profiles
of other students and wonder who might
study their wrists, have stocked up on pills,
look down from window ledges to calculate
the space between body and ground.

One Sunday afternoon with Rachel, I speak
the word that ends one story but starts another.
It's often hard to tell whether someone
doesn't want to listen or I don't want to talk.
But I feel Rachel's care.
After hugging me and posing kind questions,
she asks, *Are you in therapy?*

I'm okay. At least at this moment.

Asking for help flips what I'd been taught:

that if you suspect trouble

inside, make sure no one knows.

A Short Letter to Emily

Working our way through nineteenth-century American lit,
we don't read a woman writer until Emily Dickinson.
We can't judge another era by our standards,
the professor says. He contends that it wasn't
that women weren't capable of creative work,
but most weren't given the chance.
Okay, but I'm starting to find old words and pictures
deliberately kept from libraries and museums.

For my final paper, I read about Emily's life
and poems including "This is my letter to the World."
She favored short lines and small words
rounded like soft fists: *clover, a loaded gun, bees.*
She revised poems on cream-colored paper,
punched holes along the edges
with the needle she used for mending pockets,
then stitched together pages of poems,
choosing her own order.
She stacked the slim books like linens in a drawer.

We're instructed to separate text from writer,
but professors make exceptions for Emily and Sylvia.
I sift through speculation about whether Emily enjoyed
wild nights with a newspaperman from the nearest city,
a judge who visited from across the state,

or her best friend who was unhappily
married to her brother.
Sue lived next door, often crossing on a path
Emily called *just wide enough for two who love.*
History won't stay silent and still.
History twists out of hiding from unraveling bindings,
forgotten letters, delicate spills across margins,
a change in light making visible what was there all along.

When Emily was my age she tended her mother,
often bedridden with melancholia, neuralgia, mysteries.
She wrote, *I never had a mother....*
One to whom you hurry when you are troubled.

Dear Emily: Did you show your mother any poems?
Was she the first who never seemed to want your words?

Asking

The new women's center is in the old library
in a hall divided by makeshift walls on wheels.
A counselor listens, gasps, calls me a *survivor*,
a word whose vaguely triumphant tone
doesn't fit me any more than *victim*.
I hate answering her questions
and hate flicking them away.

I try to look composed while she misses
the point. I'm here
because I'm knocked down
by what I remember,
what I forget or mean to.
Memory doesn't just collect facts,
but insists on writing her own scripts and songs.
I find my way to the doors.

Revolutions

Shortly before the end of the semester, I find
the office of the teaching assistant of my history seminar.
He says, *You started like gangbusters, then …*

I never forgot that broken sentence.
I murmured I couldn't keep up with the reading.
But now as I try and fail to remember
what grade I got, I recall book covers:
pale red and blue on white, the French flag
on a paperback marked with my tiny notes,
and an old hardcover from a used bookstore
with folded pages that needed to be cut apart.
Remembering I ripped pages as I pushed
toward the back, I realize it wasn't the books
that made me skip classes. I spoke in that small class
and people listened. I was scared.

I'll forever mix up the French revolutions,
the various shapes of agitators' red caps,
whose throne was tossed on which bonfire,
whose heads were chopped off first.

Black Tea

Greg boils water on a hot plate in his dorm suite,
pours it into a kettle of smoky Lapsang souchong tea.
When I ask about his forestry courses, he says,
I'm going into the plant and soil concentration.
He enunciates the words as if they're a dare.
There are jobs in pest management.

You mean killing insects? You know
if they're poisoned, the birds who eat them die.

We're looking for better ways.
I'm going to need a job when I leave here.
Maybe I'll have a family to care for one day.
Or don't you think I could be a father?

I just didn't know that's what you wanted.
Though, yeah, I'm surprised.
What happened to helping trees?
And what will he have to give up to become a parent?

I put down my cup. The tea tastes like cigarettes.
Greg has a plan, like everybody but me.
Susan is graduating and got a job
teaching French in a high school.
Rachel got into a summer workshop at UMass

with a painter she says is kind of famous.
She's renting a house in Amherst with other meditators.
Another room hasn't yet been filled, she said.
You should live there, too.

I have to be older or have more credits
in order to live off campus. Besides,
I forgot to register for fall classes.

Unburied

My brother isn't in the place I still call home.
Mom tells me one of his friends heading
to California asked him to come along.
I ask, *Isn't that missing a lot of school?*

Mom shrugs.

When I was little, we saw the car our mother crashed,
learned about her fall
on the ice in front of the barber shop.
Doctors operated to shift her backbones,
which stopped the pain for a while,
then set it somewhere else.
Once, when Mom came back from the hospital,
she stayed in a bed with a crank at one end
under a canopy of poles and pulleys.
My sister, brother, and I kept our voices low,
brought toast on a tray and coffee
Mom let cool enough to drink through a straw.

Now I take a roast I won't eat from the oven,
baked potatoes I cover with broccoli and cheese.
At the dinner table I set with three plates, Mom says,
I could never get you to eat vegetables as a kid.

Maybe I should look for a therapist, I say.
Rachel told me that sometimes you don't find
the right person on the first try.

There's a pause before Dad says, *Sure.*

My mother lifts her knife, says,
I never saw what good it did to dredge up the past.
The past is here. It doesn't need digging.

Eclipsed

After Mom goes back upstairs. Dad tells me
about a time when she said pain kept her in bed.
A surgeon told her he found nothing amiss.
She insisted her back hurt too much for her to walk.
She returned to the hospital for another operation.
After the anesthesia, after my mother stood
and paced around the hospital room,
the doctor revealed he never used a knife,
proving the pain was all in her mind.
He suggested she see a psychiatrist.

Stunned by the story, I hardly notice
how my single statement of need got lost
in my parents' misery. Even I can no longer hear it.
I remember my mother finding new doctors
who believed her or at least prescribed.
If pain is in either body or mind,
she took the side of bones and muscles,
which seemed less likely to be called her own fault.

When I was twelve, Mom was bribed
into going to a different kind of hospital.
People wore regular clothes instead of hospital gowns.
They were expected to talk.
She's not crazy, our father told us.
She's afraid people think that. She's not insane.

One afternoon my father, sister, brother, and I
sat in a short row of folding chairs, stark as bones.
A woman with a clipboard on her lap
sat between my mother and us.
She asked us questions while we mostly stared.
Clearly we hadn't made our mother happy.
Any word could be used against us.
My little brother kicked a chair rung.
I was glad for the tinny sound, breaking the echo,
but Dad silenced him with a stare.

Weeks later, our mother was back by a bed
and table holding stubbed-out cigarettes
but no matchboxes, no mirrors
whose smooth surfaces could be cracked to blades.
Women must trust their reflections to others. They can't.

We watched her pack in a hurry, stuffing a box of tissues,
a used sliver of soap in her suitcase.
Her roommate urged: *Take the water pitcher!*
Take the towels. I guess they thought
they should go away with something.
Everyone's leaving, Mom said. *Everyone hates it here.*

Apprentice to Myself

I won't be a bohemian writing in a Paris garret,
but kind of like Jo March in *Little Women*,
who moved to a city to write and hand deliver stories
she hoped to sell. I study the back pages
of a newspaper for job and room listings,
find a small bedroom across or down
a hall from three others rented by old women.

Drying underwear curtains
the walls of the bathroom we share,
though we're not supposed to wash clothes in the sink.
In the kitchen I'm allotted a space in the refrigerator
to the right of a small freezer that hangs from the top.
My slim carton of milk hardens into ice.
My romaine lettuce speckles with frost.

Under a slanting ceiling, I tape the ambition bird
poem, its edges ragged where I taped it before.
I didn't bring *Ariel*, just the three sheets
of Sylvia Plath's poems I carried back from Florida.
I keep them tucked away. I unpack a notebook,
its cover paper bag brown, list books to read
and the number of pages I should write each day.

I rest an elbow on the flaking paint of the windowsill.
Maybe writing a poem can keep me

from being like my mother.
I'm sorry. That's mean.
My mother is ill.

Streets

As I unlock my bicycle chained to the porch railing,
one of the renters with hair the color of safety pins
says, *Aren't you afraid someone will snatch you off that?*

No. But the truth is that I'm scared of a lot.
Biking is better than walking, when I sometimes
pass men who make noises with pursed mouths.
I tell myself: *Don't freak out. Don't turn.*
You're fine. This is just how the world is.

I bike by neighborhoods divided by skin color,
languages, accents, particular prayers or curses.
Near the library, some people hunch,
swaddled in old blankets.
A woman steers a child to the other side of the street.
I keep pedaling past shattered glass,
a smudge of flattened feathers.

My breath stops as I recognize a man.
No. Memory is playing tricks—
memory always plays tricks.
One foot forward, one back.
Breathe in, breathe out. That rhythm.

By a Glass Door

Interviewing to be a waitress, I'm asked,
Why did you leave college?
I shrug, shift blame onto my shoulders:
I'm unfocused, unambitious.
I'll learn to hedge this question at other interviews.
Every time I see a doctor and am asked
if I've ever been hospitalized or someone
casually asks, *Have you ever been to Florida?*
I feel forced to confront or hide
from what has nothing to do with the moment.

I get the job, carry plates of hamburgers and fries.
You should hang out with us when the shop closes,
the manager says. *Make some friends.*
And I don't mean with . . . He names a girl
who rolls her eyes behind customers' backs,
delivers ice cream with an ironic swagger.

One day a little girl dances before her reflection
in the glass door, singing bits of a car commercial.
Something catches in my throat. Is it the start of a poem?

Needle and Thread

In a small shop of vintage clothes, wide-brimmed
hats with dusty feathers perch over a rack
of dresses with polka dots, shoulder pads, and stains.
A young woman stitches a button onto a sparkly sweater.
Sitting by a jar of yellow flowers as if it's a lamp,
she threads a needle, looking confident she can fix
what's missing: a button or the seam of a pocket.

As I inspect a row of denim skirts,
she explains how she cuts old blue jeans
above the knee where the fabric is most worn,
then uses that leftover cloth to stitch between
the severed jeans legs to make a skirt.
She asks if I can sew, then offers
to give me a few pairs of jeans,
pay me when I return with skirts.
I leave with borrowed shears.

Ideas and Things

I cut and stitch. I pick up a book and put it back down.
I open my notebook not because
I have something to say
but because I have something to find.
I need words and the spaces between them
to build a defense against pressures to stay silent.

I rest my fingertips on paper like it's a Ouija board.
Be patient. Keep your hands light.
I try to say too much within too many words.
My sentences turn baggy with moaning.
I remember William Carlos Williams,
a doctor who wrote poetry on the back
of prescription pads.
A white chicken, a red wheelbarrow, cold plums.
He wrote: *No ideas but in things.*

Now Close Your Eyes

On Sundays I bicycle to a meditation center
in a donated house past the edge of the city.
The young man in charge wears a white shirt,
loose trousers, and a string of coral beads.
As we sit on folding chairs or cushions,
he lights sandalwood incense, chants Sanskrit,
then switches to English to say, *Now close your eyes.*
After twenty minutes of silence, he rings a chime.
Everyone stands to talk or sip mugs of tea.

I pedal about six miles to get here,
increasingly eager to see someone named Rob,
who drives up in a black pickup truck.
His broom-colored hair grazes his shoulders.
Most of us here are soft-spoken
and hold our backs straight,
but he never looks ruffled or speaks to someone first.
His words are self-contained as hammers or wrenches.
His sentences don't tangle or sprawl
like those of people I liked in college.

Rob mentions he fought in Vietnam,
then says nothing about it except
I don't know if the war was good or bad.
Ground troops recently left Vietnam with no parades.
We think we want an ending but mean a victory.

The Driver

My landlady lives in the big house by our divided one.
She confides that she and her sister
are legally blind, asks if I have a driver's license.
If I chauffeur them in her car to go shopping once a week,
she'll pay for my lunch and give me a discount on rent.

On Saturdays, I drive the sisters to shops
in small towns, where I avoid parallel parking.
In lunch shops, I order grilled cheese
or soups dubiously vegetarian.
As we eat, my landlady talks about TV shows
or gives me advice to find nicer clothes,
pay attention to my fingernails,
go to church to meet a boy.
Divide my paycheck with a quarter for rent,
a quarter for food, another for clothes and whatnots
–does she mean books?–and the rest for savings.
You never know what will happen.

I like the fiction my landlady creates of me,
as a girl who's all right, just a little bit lost.

Different Shades of Black

The man who runs the meditation center
asks me if I can stay while he travels for a week.
My job is to answer the phone and guard
the honey jar from ants, without being too violent.
Help yourself to tomatoes from the garden,
he says. *Weed if you get a chance.*

Maybe I'll be able to write better with a green view.
Beside a window, I bend over an empty
page as if listening for a heartbeat.
I remember advice to write a poem like a letter.
You can't write one without the word *I*,
which can lead to trouble.
Once I wanted to be special. Now even
being ordinary, peaceful as jam, is a challenge.

Rob stops by one afternoon, wearing a cotton shirt,
jeans, and socks each a slightly different shade of black.
I don't remember what we talked about,
but it wasn't books or art,
Plath or Picasso, or his job working on houses.
His soft brown eyes rest on mine
as if waiting for all my stories.
Something inside me twists open.

I unlatch the screen door.

We walk past the garden and the edge of the woods.

We sit on moss and pine needles and kiss.

He stops to push back a strand of his yellow-brown hair.

He tells me about the wife who did something

horrible and left him, taking their little boy.

Before we kiss again, I fall in love

with the small boy, too, imagine

combing his hair which also falls over his eyes.

I'm ready to bake them a cake, do their wash.

I would not lose a single sock.

Back by his truck, Rob says he'll stop by tomorrow.

But he doesn't come the next day or the next.

I keep looking out the window, daydream,

build an invisible cottage from loneliness and hope.

Are Rob and his child all right?

The man who runs the meditation center returns.

He browses the notes I kept on calls,

finds ants only on the periphery of the kitchen.

He looks out the window at the overgrown garden,

then turns to rest his melancholy eyes on me. I wonder

if he didn't mean it when he told me not to mind the weeds.
Or maybe he sees that I'm sadder than when he left.

I don't see Rob again, never meet his child,
if he had one. Later, I write a poem
about someone with mismatched socks,
the only thing I know for sure.

The Coat

In the back of the vintage clothing shop,
dim as a forest, I sew on a clattering machine.
I agree to barter instead of take cash for my labor.
I browse through a rack
with winter garments the owner just hung.
A thick black coat falls wide from my shoulders,
like a tent, reaching my ankles. The heavy cloth
holds me close to earth, while the lining is silky.

Amid the racks of clothing, there's just enough room
for the restrained twirl of a girl
who wants more than she can find.

Packing Boxes

A letter needs no real introduction or conclusion,
just a knock and a wish you were here.
Summer isn't over when mail from Rachel
mentions her painting classes and a bedroom
still open in the Amherst house where she lives.
My notebook isn't half-filled with broken sentences.
I pack it in the carton with books and poems I never read.

No one seems surprised that I'm leaving the city.
Not the old women who slept in rooms by mine,
our landlady, the other waitresses, or the meditators.
Not the seamstress, quiet as cloth,
making stitches no one is meant to see.

PART III

Turning and Turning

Tangled

A Beatles song wafts from a high window
in Emily Dickinson's old home on Main Street.
Let it be … Do the caretakers ever
glimpse signs from the poet who watered plants,
stitched loose buttons, wrote on scraps
of brown wrapping paper, the backs of envelopes,
chocolate wrappers she tucked in her pockets?

Emily didn't need college. Maybe I don't either,
but I'm glad to be back in a town with big libraries,
small, beautiful bookshops. In summer,
Amherst streets cast a sense of quiet luck
to be here when many have gone.

I turn a corner toward an old farmhouse.
The handlebars of my bicycle tangle with Rachel's
and others leaning against the kitchen wall.
Cups of milk on the radiator turn into thin yogurt.
We boil then mash chickpeas to make hummus.
I rarely see the roommate who studies geology
or the guy getting a degree in premed.
A newly divorced woman is almost always around.
She offers advice to the guy who bakes brown bread,
plays an old guitar, usually pensive folk music,
in the living room by records stacked between piled bricks.

In theory we'll meditate together in late afternoon,
then have supper in the kitchen where small brown paper
bags are labeled to note various beans, seeds, and nuts.
On the bottom of a paper of typed house rules
someone has written: *No dead birds in the sink.*

Rachel tells me she's doing a series of bird paintings.
She found a crow by the road she wanted to draw
and hoped it wouldn't smell so bad if she washed it.
The cuffs of her shirt show traces of indigo paint.
Good artists don't use paint labeled black,
she says. *We mix our own from browns and blues.*
Maybe people can't see the difference,
but they can sense the layers where darkness began.

The Bell

I get a job in a stationery store. My palms
become ink smudged as I stack and sell newspapers.
In quiet moments we're supposed to dust boxes
of spooled ribbons marked to fit various typewriters,
blocks of five hundred sheets of paper I covet,
or make sure all greeting cards have matching envelopes.
Usually we just stand by the cash register and gossip.

Coming home one afternoon, I find a cast-off
typewriter for sale in a yard among broken chairs,
cartons of used textbooks, milk crates of record albums.
I set it on a wooden table in my bedroom.

The view from the window is of cornfields
and mountains, now blue-blurred by mist.
I type what I'm thinking, not much, but I want
to hear the bell that chimes at the end of each line.
A poet must be free to let everything in,
free to let everything go.
If I insist on knowing where a thought
is heading, I may never start.

A pale brown moth presses against the glass pane.
The wings curve at the tips.

Layers

Crows seem to tumble through low clouds.
I bicycle with Rachel to a UMass studio
where easels stand in front of big windows.
A radio plays the blues as a young woman
paints a picture of a rattle, baby bottle,
and stuffed rabbit on a playpen's floor.
A chatty girl paints variously shaped bread,
working fast before the colors change.
Rachel's bird is barely visible under layers.
She's lavish with turpentine, streaking, washing,
showing disappearance as much as what's there.

On some days off from work I return with Rachel.
Once, the painter-professor comes by,
stares at work on easels, grunts with tones
that students learn to interpret.
The artist-mother paints a small sandal
over the baby bottle. The rattle becomes a sippy cup,
a stuffed rabbit turns into a toy dump truck,
its shine suggesting metal.
I like seeing chances taken and abandoned,
feel privileged to see a sort of painter
I didn't find in *The History of Art.*
But why doesn't she start a new canvas
instead of painting over? Something should last.

September

The stationery store has a hopeful smell of pencils and ink.
At the counter, I often wear borrowed cardigans
or blazers Rachel's stepmother gave her: Rachel prefers
patterned skirts and knobby sweaters from Goodwill.
She took a leave from Smith to continue her series of birds,
doing independent work with her professor, Geoff.

Back home, I sit at the wooden table,
watch wild turkeys strut around old cornstalks,
their claws slender as stiletto heels.
My elbow rests near three pine cones
and a papier-mâché box of paper clips.
I start typing toward my childhood.
My mother is a diary I can't open.

A Pact

It's dark by the time I hear the kitchen door open,
shut, Rachel hooking the latch
we leave off until the last housemate is in.
I meet her in her bedroom across the hall,
fold my sweater into a pillow on the sloping plank floor.
She tells me about painting a pileated woodpecker
now stored in the back of our freezer.

As she talks too much about her professor, Geoff,
I look at postcards pinned to her wall.
A woman in a straw-seated chair, alive
with Van Gogh's slashing strokes and bold colors.
Cézanne's mountain with caramel colors, the pink
of early apple blossoms, the pale green and yellow of pears.
I ask Rachel, *Do you think you'll always paint birds?*

Maybe a garden sometime. But it won't be pretty.

Serious gardens. I can't wait to see them.

Do you think an artist can be a mother, too?
I'm afraid I won't know how.

You'll be great. My belief in Rachel
shifts into brief belief in myself.

A Short Letter to Maya Angelou

The new library rising twenty-eight stories
is surrounded by a fence so passersby can't get close
and risk being hit by bricks, which have been falling.
Inside, the floors smell new, though the worn canvas,
old glue, crumbling leather,
and the dust smell of books is stronger.
A switch unwinds as lights briefly buzz and shine.
We're not meant to linger in narrow aisles.
Books are stripped of jackets. With no photographs
or praise, I meet authors through their words.

I open *I Know Why the Caged Bird Sings*.
Maya Angelou recounts being raped
when she was eight years old. Eight.
The child tried to obey the order not to tell,
but words tumbled toward her trusted brother,
who told their mother, who mostly was missing.
The story spread. Men who believed justice
rarely came through courts
killed the monster.

No one asked what the child wanted.
She looked for sense.
Finding none, she blamed herself.
For five years, silence became a wall around her.

Dear Maya: You changed your name
from the one you had as a girl.
Building strength from love of your brother,
grandmother, teachers, and the music and light
of books, you unsettled history. You saved yourself
and girls you never knew. Thank you for writing.

Gone

A cold wind slips through cracks in the windows.
I hear the latch click closed on the kitchen door,
quick footsteps, Rachel's bedroom door shut,
crying.
I drape a blanket over my shoulders,
cross the hall, ask what's wrong.

My professor asked me to his apartment
to look at paintings. Geoff said he invited
a few other people, too. When I got there
and didn't see anyone else I got the picture.

As I touch her hand, she says, *It's okay.*
Nothing happened. I said I wanted to leave
and I left. You told me
doing this independent study with him was stupid.

I never said that.

You said it with your eyebrows.
I'll try to go back to Smith, but how can I explain
why I dropped this class? I'll look like an idiot.
I mean, asking me to come see his pictures?
They'd just say it's my fault.

But it's not. I lift the blanket
from my shoulders and fold it over her.

Mirrors, Razors, and Pens

I fill out forms to reenroll for spring semester.
The English Department advisor,
a novelist who says I should call him Paul,
tells me about Intro to Creative Writing.
You're missing some requirements,
and the class is full, but a few always drop.

I feel ready to be a student again, like Rachel,
who's back at Smith. I go to the campus
with her so she can show me the light board
in the back of the theater. A friend is teaching her
how to wield toggles to change mood and focus.
She says the person stepping into darkness
is as crucial as an actor under spotlights.
I ask, *Will you go back to painting pictures?*

I'm working on some backdrops, Rachel says.
I was never that good anyway.
And in art, it matters who sees your work.
Geoff was going to show mine to a friend
with a gallery, but that's gone now.
I mean he said he was going to do that.
Maybe he never even liked my paintings.

You *liked them.* I walk with her past dormitories,
snow shoveled to the sides of paths.
Rachel says, *Stuff like what he did happens here, too.*

It happens everywhere.

Somehow you think: Not to me.
We walk to the frozen pond, down a path beside it.
Across the ice, turrets and towers
the color of gingerbread rise over the roof
of a closed asylum once called the state hospital,
having dropped the phrase *for the insane*,
which replaced the word *lunatic*.

After Sylvia's suicide attempt, the Smith graduate
who sponsored Sylvia's scholarship sent money
so she could go to a private, pricey hospital.
Even there, staff took away keys, books,
photographs, matches, and razors.
Women couldn't light their own cigarettes
or shave their legs without a witness.
Some weren't allowed mirrors, paper, or pens.

Rachel and I walk up the hill close enough
to see boards nailed over windows. Wind howls.
Who put up the *No Trespassing* signs?
Rachel walks closer across the snow.
She speaks softly. *I never tried to save my mother.*

That's not supposed to be a child's job.

I take off my scarf, wrap it around her neck.

Her hair, the color of tea with milk, fluffs out

as she takes off her knit cap and puts it over my head.

Origins

Intro to Creative Writing is the only class
where students may write both stories and poems,
otherwise divided like sections in the library.
We sit on sofas or pillows in a big Victorian house
loaned to us Monday evenings
by one of Paul's former students.
Paul has curly hair, wayward eyebrows, a thick body,
and a soft accent from somewhere near New York City.
He says, *We'll do some exercises in class.*
You can develop them at home to turn in next week.
The first prompt: write about a time you loved writing.

He wants us to write here, now,
in front of strangers? Is he kidding?

Not prizes or crap like that, Paul adds.
Let your hand and mind be free
without worrying what's good or bad. Go.

I remember studying phonics and the small
powerful life of punctuation in second grade.
Cards with twenty-six letters wreathed the room.
Children tilted pencils to assigned angles,
filled sheets of paper repeating letters.
At recess, two friends and I sometimes stayed

inside to cut and fold arithmetic paper
into small books. We shared crayons
and consulted one another on spelling.
We carried the folded books in our hands
like small, soft animals to our teacher.
She held a stapler like a chalice.

Paul says, *Time,* then poses the next prompt:
What made you feel you're not a writer?

Everything Made Me Stop

Anything can swerve, rip into memory, which shifts
like a gangly bird caught beneath my rib bones.
I find my way to fifth grade, when again I wrote,
now silently and alone, at recess held indoors in winter.
Until the teacher called me to her big desk,
told me writing wasn't a choice at recess.
I could do puzzles, play hangman or tic-tac-toe
at the blackboard, or join the girls
who gathered around her, cooing at her sparkly ring,
asking about her upcoming wedding.
Was she afraid I was writing something hurtful,
like Harriet the Spy, or did she crave another admirer?

That year I wasn't living at home
or with Diane, whose mother just had a baby,
which my mother disapprovingly called a surprise.
My mother arranged for me to live with Louise,
who was a year older. We weren't friends,
though I knew her from church and Girl Scouts.
She had more badges than I did
and hers were neatly stitched on a green sash.
Her grades were better than mine,
which I knew because she told me.
I wore skirts handed down from my sister
that failed to stay quite at my waist despite safety pins.

Louise won prizes for good grooming
at Friday night ballroom dancing class.
The main rule at her house was the rule
at home, but bigger: don't be trouble.

The Man in the Chair

On Saturdays, sometimes we bicycled past woods,
cows grazing in meadows, crows flying over cornfields.
Once, Louise stopped her bike at a crossroads
before a small shop that stood alone,
unlike the row of attached stores in town
where I knew the names of people who worked there.
I stood, straddling my bike, said, *I'll wait here.*

But after waiting felt long, I opened the door.
The stacked cans, boxes of cereal,
rows of amber, brown, and clear bottles looked dusty.
A man sat on an old stuffed chair.
He was round in the middle like a fish
with a pouting mouth, big eyes, pale skin.
Large as he was, he seemed without muscle,
but might be suspended as if underwater.
Bottles of sodas bobbed in an open cooler.
Seeing me look, the man said, *Help yourself.*

I said I had to go. Let him think I wasn't thirsty.
I didn't care if anyone thought I was afraid.
Nobody argued. Louise stayed.
She never suggested I go back.
We're told to be quiet
until we no longer must be told.

Divided Language

In Poetry after World War II, we read work by writers
critical of the military, capitalism, and conformity.
Allen Ginsberg opened doors to writing about anything.
In "Kaddish," he laments
his mother's decades in an asylum.
He spent less time in one.
"Howl" begins: *I saw the best minds*
of my generation destroyed by madness.

No one calls his poems confessional,
a word that seems reserved for women
like Anne Sexton, who wrote "The Ambition Bird."
A boy named Ron says, *She wrote outrageous*
things just for attention. Poor whiny me.
He tugs the cuff of his paisley shirt.
But she's not as bad as Sylvia Plath and that belly jar book.
Plath's fans are obsessed with death.
Why should we read about people who killed themselves?
His voice holds venom I don't hear for Van Gogh,
whose rough life ended with gunshot.
The artist's advocates are quicker to fault
the world that didn't pay enough attention.

Sylvia Plath was talented, the professor tells
the class of thirty or so students.
But her work is marred by anger.

I look sideways at Pat,
who's small and wears large clothes.
She sits in a back row near me and Michael,
whose curly hair has the slight shine of raisins.
He and I often exchange glances
that stay short of eye rolls, then talk after class
about poems that make us want to write.

Sure, the girl in some Plath poems is not nice.
She snaps apart a string of pearls,
peels off her white gloves and chews them.
But the professor can't get over the line
in "Lady Lazarus" about eating men like air.
Meanwhile, we're all expected to swallow
words about men's violence, pretend
it's not personal, it's literature.

I don't want to read about problems
with boyfriends or bodies, Ron says.
It's embarrassing. Nobody wants to know.

I want to know. But even now as I write,
I hear: *Nobody wants to know.*
Again and again, I try to stop the words.

Broken World

I pull off my boots, drop my coat in a pile.
Paul asks us to write something set in a kitchen.
I like reading fiction set near sinks and ovens
where sisters or kindred spirits sweep, scrub,
confide dreams they couldn't speak elsewhere.
But my mother keeps threatening to enter
and I'm not ready. I'm relieved when Paul says:
Now write about a moment when life changed.
Something lost, something gained. Is that every story?
Maybe being on the edge of a new-to-someone world.

Past potted plants, the windows are darkened to mirror.
My stomach waves as if I'm falling.
Was this how Demeter's daughter felt
when the earth split open and she tumbled
through a crack to the underworld?

Dear Persephone: Nobody grabbed your hands.
Your mother didn't come around till later,
then snatched rose petals, leaving thorny briars.
She turned grasses brown and brittle,
called for an end to perpetual summer,
created winter, all to be with you half the time.
The best a raped girl can hope for is compromise.

Who set the rule that you couldn't leave
the underworld if you ate?
You were hungry as any girl.
Tasted seven seeds, pale red and sticky, not that good.
When you came back aboveground,
did daylight seem glaring?
Did you feel always an outsider, walking
under blue sky, then back to stumbling in the dark?

There's never an ending. We all circle back,
swallowing anger, spitting it up.
Often hungry, scared to taste sweet, sticky seeds,
anything, lest something small
plunges us further into a broken world.

Puzzles

In Poetry after World War II, we choose poets
for a final paper. Pat, who rarely speaks
or even lifts her head, names Maya Angelou.

She writes about rainbows, Ron scoffs.
Not real ones, but slogans. It's not poetry, but message.

I like Maya Angelou. My voice wobbles.
I don't know how to say she dared to scrape through
what's broken and find not just blood but light.
I glance at Pat, who leans
so her hair drapes over her face,
her big shirt slants over her chest.

*Poems don't have to be puzzles packed
with hidden meaning to be great,* Michael says.

After class, I walk through the hall with him.
Of course Ron would dismiss Maya Angelou, he says.
He can only like a poet who stays misunderstood.

*The idea that you can be talented and also famous
wrecks the notion that really good poets,
maybe like him, are bound to be passed over.*

Michael nods. He wears an old woolen jacket and jeans.
His belly slightly curves under his button-down shirt.
He discusses a poem's balance of fog and glare,
parses what he admires in Maya's poems
and what he doesn't.
Then tells me his final paper will focus on Frank O'Hara,
whose poems are often shaped by what's left of a day,
some lines connecting trashy magazines and ballet.
Frank O'Hara puts a story in a short space, listing
what happened, and what happened next, until
holy moly the ordinary becomes sublime.

Who are you writing about? Michael asks.

I don't know. I like how Anne Sexton's work
has both the pull of stories and shine of poems.
I feel loyal to Sylvia Plath, but kind of want
to keep what's between us confidential. I sidestep.
I haven't written a long paper in a while.
My one on Emily Dickinson got out of control.

Emily Dickinson can make that happen.
Michael's dark hair is short, but ragged around his ears.
Have you been to her house?

*Not yet. I live nearby, but never remember
which days it's open.* Why would I want to see
her desk or the pantry where she wrote poems
on the backs of recipes? Seeing the outside
of Sylvia's dorm didn't help me, did it?

Ambitions

After the last writing class, Paul asks me
to meet him in a small book-lined room on the side
of the Undergraduate English Department main office.
He digs through a file and pulls out my transcript.
There are some gaps. His forehead wrinkles.
*This is the only writing class I teach, but I can
see if I can get you into one of the fiction workshops.*

I thought I'd start with a poetry workshop.

Those fill up even faster, Paul says. *People think
since poems are shorter, they take less time to write.*
We talk some more about my goals. I thank him,
then go into the main office, where Michael
is chatting with Jude, who oversees two phones,
a typewriter, a coffee pot, and stacks of paper.

Michael walks with me outside the building.
Recently, we talked about characters
in books and I found I was speaking of myself.
But today my face feels heavy, my mouth stuck.
Under an enormous tree, Michael asks, *Is something wrong?*

*Paul just said he'd try to sign me up
for a fiction writing class. Not that I call*

myself a poet, but I do better writing short.
What's left off the page matters.
And I'm not sure I can write many pages
all the way to the margins
without getting caught in memory's nets.

He shouldn't tell you what to do,
Michael says. *He's kind of nosy.*

He's an advisor. It's his job to ask questions.

You should take poetry with Professor Clark.
He seems stuffy, but you'll get a good background in forms.

I've read some of Professor Clark's rhyming poems
looking back at his service in World War II
or odes to nature, narrated by someone
who doesn't worry about men lurking in woods,
or turning back to be on time for work,
or how much rice might be in the kitchen,
and perhaps beans, broccoli, and an egg.
I'm not keen to work with him, but only three poets
teach in the creative writing faculty composed
entirely of White men, though we just call them professors.
Clark may be better than Finn, whose poems

seem like mazes or dark tents only a few may enter.
A smirk often nests in a scraggly beard.
His jeans bag into unlaced work boots.

Michael stops by a bench, shrugs off
his knapsack and pulls out a paper.
Could I show you one of my poems?

I nod and read his short poem
about Beethoven knocking candles off a piano,
punching a choirboy who got the music wrong.
I like the history in it, I say. *The style reminds me
of Frank O'Hara's, with details and fast lines.*

Michael's face widens with a smile he holds back.
I keep my smile tucked in, too, then add,
*But I didn't realize Beethoven was so miserable.
I don't think art needs to come from pain.*

*Beethoven didn't have it easy.
None of his loves worked out. The "Ode to Joy" took him
thirty years to get right. And by then he was deaf.*
Michael slips the poem back in his knapsack.
Anyway, do you have summer plans?

After I say I'll be working and writing, Michael says,
My father doesn't really have anyone in his life now.
He wants me to drive with him to Canada.
His round face brightens. *There's a big Shakespeare festival.*
And Toronto has some great bookstores.

You'll like that. My voice sounds too low.
He has a parent who wants to spend time with him.
He understands Shakespeare.
He won't be taking on extra hours in a stationery store.

I'd like to see you when I get back, he says.
Would you give me your phone number?

I write the number at our house in the notebook
he opens. He slips it back in his knapsack and grins.
Professor Clark told me I should write
while I'm traveling and that he'll look at what I've done.
I don't know if I can take another class with him,
so his offer to review poems is really something.

That's great. My voice sounds flat,
but Michael doesn't seem to notice.

He says, *If Clark thinks I have talent, maybe*
I can convince my dad it would be a good
investment for me to go to grad school in writing.

I'm happy for you. It's stupid
to be jealous, but it rises between us
in a brief, awkward hug goodbye.

The Brick House on Main Street

The sky is a pale blue envelope.
I walk past restaurants, bookshops, a man
in front of the post office yelling to no one
or the world. I head down the hill.
I just got a letter from my old roommate Susan
who doesn't love teaching French,
but liked codirecting the high school play.
This summer she's driving out west with a friend.
Rachel is graduating and found a job in a small theater,
which kind of sounds like selling tickets,
living with her grandmother in New York.
Everybody but me is changing, doing something.

A sign in front of Emily Dickinson's house
says *Open.* I gather with a few people in the parlor.
The guide scrolls through family names and dates.
Is it real? a woman asks of the rugs, the furniture.
The guide explains decisions about reproductions,
tells us that after Emily took on some care
of her mother, she seldom left the house and garden.
Emily knew people in town gossiped,
called her the Myth. Did she like or hate that?

At the top of the stairs a white dress
is displayed on a mannequin without a head.

I study the pocket just big enough
for a pencil and scrap of paper.
Who stitched all that lace by the collar, cuffs,
twelve tiny buttons placed precisely as words?

We crush toward the bedroom doorway.
Is it real? a woman asks of the coverlet and wallpaper.
I stare at the little table by the window
as the guide moves down the hall and ends the tour.
I want to see Emily's hands holding a pen,
want to step over the braided cord
to touch the chair that knew her back.

As I leave the house, pass the picket fence,
my face feels more like glass than skin.
I walk down the hill past lilacs
whose blossoms are brown and stiff as paper.
I don't want to drive with a sad father
across Canada and clap at the end of *Hamlet.*
I don't care much about seeing the Grand Canyon.
I don't want to look for jobs in New York theaters.
But I want something. I want, I want,
I want to write, giving
what's here a chance
to live again.

I want to find courage to wrestle out
what hunkers inside me
like a wounded bird flapping, ruffling wings.
I feel the pinch of a beak, the prickle of feathers.
Something is caught in my throat,
but I don't open my mouth.

PART IV

Telling

Kinds of Courage

Books with dark spines look pasted on shelves.
A man with clipped hair the color
of the steel file cabinets speaks a cold language.
I leave the university health care building,
return to the women's center in the old library.
I hope no one recognizes me as the girl
who was once called a survivor
and left here with no thanks or explanation.
I pass posters of the women's symbol with a fist,
suffragists waving banners,
mill workers or factory girls on strike,
Harriet Tubman holding a rifle, and present-day women
wearing hard hats, tool belts, balancing on steel rails.
Maybe the defiant women never meant to reproach me,
measure who deserves to be called brave.

Lost Girls

I leave with a short list of graduate students
in social work whose small fees are on a sliding scale.
I call a therapist who praises me for doing okay.
I suppose she hoped her steady voice
would instill trust, but it marks a distance between us.

I meet another woman in a basement room
of a big house. The walls smell of new paint.
Ellen's body is tight as an athlete's.
Lines in her sunbaked skin fan from her eyes.
She looks ready to run a marathon,
but perches on a rocker as she reads a poem:
Márgarét, áre you gríeving
Over Goldengrove unleaving?

The poem is sad with no one trying to fix it.
Leaves fall
and rot
and disappear.
I weep for the girl who misses childhood
or maybe the girl who walked
in the wrong place and lost
not just who she was that morning
but everyone she was before.

On My Way Back

Ellen puts down the last poem read in this room.
Speaking softly enough for me to hear,
she asks: *What do you remember?*
She spreads her arms as if stretching muscles,
ready for work. She stays close, quiet,
then and on coming Wednesday mornings
as I creep toward what's not far
enough behind me.
Where does a story start?

We circle back to when my sister and I
were in high school and at the dinner table.
My sister said it was a bad idea
for our church youth group to invite kids
from a church in the city
to come talk with us and eat pizza.
What are they going to say, um, nice church?
Are we supposed to ask, So what is it like to be Black?

Our father protested it was just a chance
to get to know each other. *In one night, Dad?*
My sister's voice scraped. *What right*
do we have to ask them to teach us,
but not really, then go back home?

I remembered her words but forgot
when my college roommate urged me to sign up
for a program where we'd walk through
a neighborhood to learn about other people.
Rather than wear a peasant blouse, jeans,
or Indian print skirt, that morning I fastened a hook
at the collar of a brown-and-green plaid dress.
It looked like something worn to a science fair,
left behind in my sister's closet
when she went away to college.

I carried a bag just big enough
for a thin wallet with a few dollar bills,
a ballpoint pen, and notebook like the one
Harriet the Spy kept in her pocket.
I meant to observe, maybe take notes, like a writer.

Be Polite

My stories stutter, skid, slam, lengthen,
shrink, then spread in Ellen's office.
Every memory, whether image or story,
offers a new place to begin and end.
I remember
strolling past a diner, a tailor shop,
homes with small yards.
A few adults walk, hunched under the heat.
Some glance at me,
the only person on the street who's White.

My voice cracks as I describe
the young man who doesn't ask,
Where are you from?
He knows I'm not from here.
He asks, *Where you going?*
I shake my head, walking with him
now beside me. I don't want him to think
I want to get away because he's Black.
But as his arm presses mine,
I take longer, faster steps,
apologize for my hurry.

He keeps up, stays close, closer, still talking.
I start to sprint.
He grabs my wrist, turns it hard,
splits my life into before and ever-after.

Falling

Stop! Someone is waiting for me.
My words are pitched high,
desperate to show I'm not alone.
I'd never been taught to fight, but to beg.
As if this were a movie,
I try to show someone I'm human, too.
He'll wonder where I am.
He's looking for me. I wish that were true.
The professor who dropped me off,
after leaving three other students alone elsewhere,
isn't due to pick me up for a few more hours.

The young man's hand tightens.
Maybe he knows I'm a liar.
Let me go! Maybe I say, *Please,*
before shouting for help.

A few people pass, glance, then away,
like those who might have seen
a boy with wax wings on fire falling.
Sheep graze. Men fish or guide a plow.
The stranger presses a hand over my mouth.

A door opens. I yell, *Help me,*
to a plump woman with a tightening mouth.
Call the police! Please! The door shuts.

Not a Gift

One July morning in the basement room,
Ellen coaxes me to scream
as I had when the man twisted back
my hair, tugged it like a leash.
With his other hand he wrenched
my arm behind his back.

Ellen braces a pillow before her.
She asks me to punch hard,
to find the ache and muscle
nice girls weren't taught to know.

The bird once stuck in my chest and throat
bangs its wings as I remember
being pulled past weeds behind a church.
The man pushes my back to the ground,
his body pinning down mine.
He lifts the skirt of the plaid dress.
My single half-prayer is to live,
laced with expectation that I won't.
He thrusts as if he owns the sun and sky
and I am dirt, stepped on, gone into specks.
His body rises and lowers
for a few minutes, forever

before his arms unlock me.

He stands, buckles his belt,

says, *Don't tell or I'll kill you.*

He picks up my bag, slides out the wallet,

holds it toward me

as if asking for permission to take it.

Blue

No wind stirs. Grasses rustle only
because the man brushes them as he walks off.
I bend for my bag with the pen and notebook.
I stand still, alive, listening
to birds and distant traffic.
The sky seems to move toward
me as if ready to listen.
What's above was never so blue.

Transparent

I make my way down a sidewalk, spot a phone booth,
duck inside, grab the sleek receiver.
Anyone could see through these clear walls
and guess I was going to tell.

Maybe I'll be killed.
The phone stays silent by my ear.
I reach into my bag and remember
I don't have a dime to call for help.
I bend under the force of my tears,
grieving the missing coin.

When I exit the booth, a passerby scowls
at the blood dripping and drying on my legs.
His lips purse as if he might spit.

Gone

Trucks and sedans pass before a police car stops.
Two men step out, glance at the red streaks
on my legs and sandals, then pull up their gazes.
For the first time I speak the word *rape*.
I hear the word as if from a distance.
A scrap of silence falls afterward, reminding me
of speaking for the first time words I'd read,
just before my sister mocked my mispronunciation.

We'll take you to the hospital to get checked,
but first can you show us where it happened?
Ordered to get in the car,
I touch the front door handle.
A policeman clears his throat,
tells me to get in the back.
Alone,
I keep my head down as we pass
homes where someone might be making coffee
or a peanut butter sandwich.
Someone might look in a mirror,
deciding what to wear.
Someone might be crying.
I guide the police to the churchyard
to witness grasses battered as if by a storm.
One officer wanders with eyes down, snaps pictures.

He returns with my soft, thin wallet.

He asks, *Was this empty?*

No. There were some bills. Gone now.

The man who took the wallet didn't even want it.

Evidence

I'm handed a flimsy robe,
told to take off all my clothes.
I wrangle myself onto a high, narrow cot
in a hospital room.
A sheet is draped over me.
I'm commanded to slip my feet into holsters,
spread my legs for a doctor
who scrapes and swabs for evidence.
My body becomes a map as he charts bruises,
plucks hair–mine, his–
extracts blood and semen from parts of myself
I hadn't yet learned to name.

Truth and Consequences

I'm the scene of a crime, still as a ditch.
The police return as if from a colloquium in the hall.
The doctor gives them his findings.
Samples of me are discussed.
After the doctor leaves, the police say they have questions.
They're taller than me and look
as if they work on their muscles as an art.
I don't want to sound like a needy child
and ask for a blanket, but say, *I'm cold.*

You're hot, actually. The doctor said you have a fever.
The police pepper me with questions
that divide the world between right and wrong,
perp and victim, man and woman,
Black and White, North and South,
lies and truth, who might win or lose in court.
The questions set a world of fault, measure:
How loud did you scream? How fast did you run?

One man parses my use of the word *dragged*,
asks me to mime how my hair was pulled back.
There's no room for anything that falls
outside the lines their questions frame.
One man asks, *What were you doing in the city?*

Wait till you hear this. One of the policemen
I first met tilts words like a table,
slides me to the subject of the sentence.
As I say the word *college*, the men glance
at each other, eyebrows slightly up.
I'm in shock, but I can still see.

Alone? He repeats the word
as if no one had been that stupid
since Little Red Riding Hood took her time,
then tried to talk her way out of trouble.

Questions meant to solve a crime
or assess whether I deserve help
repeat like those about the girl wearing the red hood.
Should she have stepped off the path,
picked flowers, and daydreamed?

Yes, yes, yes.
She saw the bees and thorns, that liar watching,
but she wanted to go where she wanted to go.
She deserved to both leave the path and reach a safe house.

Did He Have a Weapon?

I shake my head, hating to offer the wrong answer.
They seem to gauge my belief that I'd be murdered
as evidence of my stupidity or innocence.
No one had ever threatened to kill me.
I didn't think to ask how.

A man asks, *Why didn't you fight more?*

No one ever taught me to punch, kick,
bite, use fists, fingernails, feet, or teeth as weapons.
Flight was my choice, hiding,
to save me from the worst or the next to worst.
Niceness was a tactic, seeming compliance,
like the warnings I'd had
about mugging: swap a wallet for your life.

The police leave. A nurse helps me
onto a gurney, covers me with sheets
so tightly tucked I can't sit or run.
My eyes stay on the ceiling as I'm wheeled to a hall.

A man who must know I can't see him,
but I can hear him, says, *If this happened
to my daughter, she would've been killed
before she let him do that.*

Putting Together a Girl

The girl on the gurney is pushed to a large room,
then past rows of beds like those
in *Madeline* when she gets her appendix out.
There's no shape of a rabbit on the ceiling.
Steel rods clang as a curtain is drawn.

A nurse ducks through with a trolley stacked
with white washcloths, linens, a bowl of water.
I politely protest I can wash myself.
She says, *Let me.*
She untucks the tight sheet,
drapes a new one lightly over me
that she shifts as she dips a cloth in warm water.

Silently stroking, she gives me back my body
one wrist,
ankle,
heel,
toe,
sole at a time. She checks the water for warmth,
smooths together bruised skin, muscles, bone, and spirit.
Working slowly as if I might memorize tenderness,
she folds sheets back and under, like waves of water.

Baskets

In the room where the paint no longer smells fresh,
Ellen turns back the clocks, sets them on pause.
She holds wide baskets of time
while I search for the right or wrong words.
For the first time I don't feel rushed
or worry, much, about whether I'll upset the listener.
Memories I never meant to keep,
stronger than those I strived to save,
slam through the room.

I remember: A policeman says,
In Florida rape means the death penalty.
Do you believe in that?
The question is like those discussed
in English class or church.
There are only ten commandments
and one seems particularly clear.
I shake my head.
I don't believe in the death penalty.

She's from Massachusetts, one man explains.
Next month, it will become the nation's
lone blue state during presidential elections,
with the majority voting for a candidate
we hoped would end the war in Vietnam.

A policeman scowls.
Do you want criminals running free?

I don't want anyone else to be hurt.

Then he must be punished. The policeman's
eyebrows lift as if shaping a picture of me
holding up two fingers in a peace sign.
I become the hippie girl from New England,
a vegetarian who refused to dissect frogs in biology class.
Me, but with many parts missing.

A Student of Silence

In a room with a view of the hospital parking lot,
a girl a little older than me stands by one of two beds.
She wears a terry-cloth bathrobe,
its belt neatly pulled and tied.
Whatever brought her here, she was prepared.
We exchange a few polite words,
as if I'm meeting someone at college.

Soon two policemen enter. One holds
a small batch of photographs he shows me.
As I say, no, no, no, the men twist their lips.
They take big breaths as if letting go
of the trust in me they first had
because I accused a stranger, not someone I knew.
I was White and eighteen, not too young nor too old.
It was daylight. Girls may walk outdoors at noon.
I was good enough, smart enough,
neither too calm nor too emotional,
polite, sober, and wearing a prim dress,
though prim can be provocative.
Anything can be provocative.
Anything can be called the victim's fault.

When the men leave, my roommate asks,
Why didn't you tell me what happened?

I shrug, shift my eyes.

Because I am beginning the work of not telling.

Because it would be terrible if she cared or if she didn't.

I hadn't wondered why she was in the hospital.

She looked all right. She looked better than me,

but I forgot how much seeing can't tell.

Distance

When my father walks through
the ever-open door of the hospital room,
I swing my legs off the bed but don't stand.
I put a hand behind my back,
grapple with my gaping robe.
My bones seem to be missing,
though I suppose the sense of absence
comes from my sore muscles.

Dad's gaze lands on me, then my roommate.
His smile is too big, his mouth hard,
maybe to keep his face from collapsing.
He sways slightly as he halts
two or three arm's-lengths away from me.
My father may have had a hundred reasons
to stop there. But when I'm rendered untouchable,
I understand the worst might not be over.

Dad hands me a piece of lined notebook paper,
the edges ragged where torn from a wire spiral.
Your mother is sorry she couldn't come.
She asked me to give this to you.

Evidence

The next morning, two policemen stride
through the stark room's open door.
Speaking about keeping my dress
for evidence, one hands me a paper bag
that holds clothing from the women's prison:
a pair of slacks and a white shirt printed
in block letters with the prison's name.
I used to tell that as if it were funny.

They show me a second batch of photographs.
Maybe with some they showed already.
My memory of that body turned to weapon
doesn't match the framed, still faces.
I say, *I don't see him.*

The men look at each other. One says,
She won't say because she doesn't want
him to be executed. She told us that.

The other nods. *Some people, especially in the North,*
can't tell one Black person from another.

I don't want to be *some people*, but
I probably am. I've mismatched
Black singers and actors in uncaptioned photos.

A change in haircut, clothing, lighting throws me off.
A writer should be observant, but even recently
I failed to recognize the blond, freckled mailman
when he was out of uniform. Often I can't tell
one yellow dog or bald baby from another.

A policeman clears his throat, looks at me,
Are you sure?
I'm not sure of much.
Except that I cannot say I see
the man I remember in my gut and bones.
On my back, I believed I was memorizing his face,
but maybe I was already starting to forget.

The policeman slides the photographs in his pocket.
I can't always know who hurt me.
Maybe I failed to identify the rapist.
Or the police never found him,
never offered the right picture.
Busy with new calls and crimes,
did they turn their backs
when they saw little on their side? I don't know.

Susan told me most rape cases don't go to trial.
I read that *most* is calculated

at about ninety-five out of a hundred.
I don't know what loads are carried
by the five who made it all the way to trials,
but I'm sure they're not light.
Most of us feel bound by a story with no ending.
Quiet as ghosts, we make our bodies into a courthouse
where we're not only victim, but judge, jury, lawyers.
We carry invisible handcuffs, gavel, notebook,
memorize every question and instruction.
Why didn't you try harder to run?
Why didn't you scream louder, longer?
Keep your answers calm and brief.

Trust

The shriveled stalks of lilacs,
petals gone, wave like small ghosts
on the bush by the door of our old farmhouse.
Summer is almost over and I haven't written one poem.

I open my notebook on the back steps by the mailbox,
look past the empty gravel lot to wild grasses and flowers.
Birds rustle. Bees drone and hum.
My gaze lands on thistles.
Purple tufts reign over sharp-edged leaves.
I fetch a glass jar from the kitchen, shears,
and an oven mitt I wrap around the prickly stem.
Then spring back, stung, indignant
that a bee chose my arm
when I long honored their freedom,
praised their gifts of honey and pollination.

By the time I make and dab on a paste
of baking soda and water, the pain is minor.
But maybe the back steps are no place for a poem.
I return to my bedroom, where the bottle
of Florida sand, seashells, and water has gone murky.
The girl who took Rachel's room seems
to be falling for the boy who plays the guitar.
I don't really like them or the other meditators that much.

The bookkeeper at the stationery store
tells me she converted her garage to an apartment
and the woman who lives there just lost her roommate.
The two bedrooms are small
and the view is of the driveway,
but it's closer to both work and the university.
She has a dog she'd like me to watch when she travels.

I leave the windowsill of my new room bare,
but prop postcards against a wall.
They curl like petals in the late summer's heat.
Cézanne's mountain breaking or coming together.
He never gets what he sees quite right, but tries again.

My old roommate Susan sent a black-and-white photograph
of an edge of a Navajo rug from the Grand Canyon.
She wrote that a broken line in the weaving
may mark a shift from boredom to awe.
This doesn't seem like something Susan would say.
Maybe she was told this by the girl
traveling with her. Maybe they fell in love.
Would she tell me? That would be nice.
Or maybe it just seemed stupid to send a postcard
of even a tiny slice of the Grand Canyon,
which I do want to see for myself. I want, I want.

The Scent of Old Leaves

Memories break unbidden as dreams and nightmares.
But in the English office I greet Paul and Jude,
the young woman who runs things,
as if I'm a regular person with regular goals.
I learn the fiction seminar I signed up
for was moved to spring semester.
What's the point of being here if I'm not writing
or trying to write? Or am I relieved?

I head down the dim hall and see Michael.
His hair, like a blackboard with more dust
than shine, is cut so short it barely curls.
He stops, shifts his weight between his feet,
asks, *How was your summer?*

Mostly working. I went to the Emily Dickinson house.

Michael frowns. Does he guess I'm leaving
out a lot? Or is he mad I went to Emily's house without him?
It wasn't that interesting, I say.
Except for the white dress. *How was Canada?*
Did you like the Shakespeare plays?

He nods. *I tried calling you when I got back.*
Someone said you'd moved and he'd take the message.

I look to the side. I said I'd go back to that house,
but never did. *I lost track of things after I moved.*

He shrugs. I know it doesn't sound true
and it certainly isn't the whole truth.
I ask, *How did your meetings with Clark go?*

He replies, *Not great.*

I shake my head, but don't have much sympathy.
Michael isn't a boasting sort, but guys get used to praise.
I suppose Clark didn't give him enough.
But you're still writing?

Not much. I'm starting courses
leading to teaching high school.

As I watch him walk away, his wool jacket skims
his butt. A little *V* that opens wider with each step.
Can't someone becoming a teacher still write poems?

Work

That fall I often oversleep, go to the library
between classes and lose track of time.
I'm exhausted from looking for a way out of a story
that moves backward more than forward.
Often I can't muster energy to get to and cross campus,
but I go to work. I need the folded bills and coins
that come in a small pumpkin-colored envelope
with a handwritten tally of my hours that week.

In the shop that smells of paper, ink, tobacco,
a new employee grins as he enters the door.
Will lifts his bicycle over his shoulders
on his way to stash it in the back room.
A man in a long, ripped coat walks to the counter,
asks me, *Do you know Emily Dickinson?*
When I don't reply, he says, *She was so sad.*
She died of that. She hanged herself.

I say, *No, she didn't.*
I hate this town. I love this town.

Another Fall

Maple leaves bleed red. Oak leaves turn brittle.
The world is breaking, or is that me?
The Victorian novel course was a bad idea.
Those books are thick.
I'm sick of deciding what's good, what's not,
as if beauty isn't in the eye of beholder after all.
I drop a class, then get a notice
that my financial aid is being canceled.
I stop at the English office, confide in Jude,
who sets aside the course catalogs she's collating.
She insists I talk to Paul. *That's what he's here for.*

I try not to cry as I explain the problem
though not the details of how memory
burns my skin, runs like a blade under my knees.
Paul offers to give me credits for an independent study.
I shake my head. *I'm writing, but nothing good.*

Most important work starts out as bad, he says.
I won't read it unless you want me to.
Just stop by every few weeks to check in.

I'm grateful, all the mess of me, for this chance.
Then about two weeks later, when leaves have fallen,
Jude finds me and leads me back to the English office.

Paul offers me a work-study job. He says,
We got approved to hire someone to help out
in the office for ten or twenty hours a week.
You could keep your job in town.

Saved

In the English office I assist students filling out forms,
sort mail, tape up posters announcing poetry readings.
I answer simple questions about class schedules
and requirements or chat as students wait to see Paul.
Sometimes I say something that makes someone smile.

In Jude's free time, she works on organizing
a union of clerical workers, the phrase
she taught me to use instead of secretary.
When she's out of the office, I sit at her desk
facing the door to greet students or professors coming in.
Paul told me I should write when my tasks are done,
but I work on homework. Maybe I should become
one of the English majors who read and write papers
instead of poems. Most don't seem as bruised.

I rummage through a clay bowl Jude filled
with old political buttons about war protests,
boycotts to help farmers, and support for Earth Day.
One shows a wire hanger with a line crossed through it.
I remember a girl who disappeared from high school,
then returned looking thin and sad,
saying she spent the winter with an ill aunt.
When *Roe v. Wade* recently made abortion legal,
I remembered how anxiously I waited

for the return of my period after I was raped.

Memory doesn't follow calendars or clocks.

I stir the saved buttons.

Civilization doesn't follow a straight line.

Starry Nights

One afternoon Michael comes into the office.
He, Jude, and I talk about Sylvia Plath.
It's sad that she killed herself, Michael says.
And Anne Sexton in her sealed-up garage.
Virginia Woolf wading with rocks in her pockets.

Not every woman writer kills herself, I say.
People paint blame like a flag:
this could never happen to me.
Everybody likes that starry, starry night song.

Michael softly sings Don McLean lyrics:
"But I could have told you, Vincent
This world was never meant for one
As beautiful as you." I see what you mean.
I guess he's treated differently because he's a guy.

I don't want to know the details of how Sylvia's life ended.
I don't want to argue with a guy I like.
Anger is a half-hidden safety pin.
Can I ever become an ordinary person who writes?

Colorful Erasers

Someone about my age comes into the office
with a girl who looks just old enough to be in school,
which might be closed today for snow.
Paul opens the door to his side office,
waves in the student, who tells the little girl
to sit on the floor by a low table.

I clear away coffee cups and papers,
miffed as if I were asked to watch the child
while her mother and Paul discuss writing.
But the girl doesn't need minding.
She removes a pencil and paper
from her backpack printed with ladybugs.
She lines up erasers shaped like animals.

When the side door opens, Paul introduces me
to Deborah: *Two of our best writers!*
You should exchange work.
Deborah's smile is tight. She nods
at the little girl with dark, wavy hair like hers.
She's already packing pink, yellow, and blue erasers,
gathering her rustling jacket, sleek as a parachute.

The Gift

In December, face flushed from the cold,
Will ferries his bicycle to the back of the stationery store.
I learned he's on the high school track team.
He jokes with the paperboys and politely but pointedly
checks the bigoted words of an older clerk.
In a lull at the cash register, he confides
his doubts about going to UMass next year,
though it's free since his father teaches there.

It's big, but then you find your few people.
I probably sound old, which is okay.
He's too young to be asking me to go with him to a movie.
Even if he were older, I wouldn't want to go out
with someone in the store whom everyone would discuss.

The owner gives me the usual slip with the dates
and times when I'm due to work the coming week.
I see I'm scheduled for the afternoon of Christmas Eve.
I lead people wearing thick coats and wet boots
to possible presents, Amherst College sweatshirts
or stationery textured like a lake rippled
by a slight breeze, too thick to crumple.
I wipe back tears because I won't be able
to get home for Christmas
and because I don't want to.

I return to the register. Will asks me what's wrong.
He disappears after I tell him, guiding
a customer to sports equipment in a back room.
Old men ask for packs
of cigarettes shelved behind my back.
Children solemnly survey candy packed in boxes
or balanced in rows. One makes his choice,
peels off his mittens, reaches to spill coins
on the newspaper stacks. We puzzle out the math.

Will returns to my side and says he told
the owner he'd take my Christmas Eve shift.
I thank him. He says, *It's no big deal.*
When I'm done, I'll just go home across town.

Green

Chipped angels and balls stripped of glitter
are nestled in crumpled old newspapers.
Probably the last good holiday was when I was ten.
Mom gave me a turquoise shirt I'd shown her
in the Sears catalog. Dad gave me two books
from the used bookstore: autobiographies
by Helen Keller and Eleanor Roosevelt,
legends who triumphed despite disappearing mothers.
The books were too old for me, but I was happy
my father noticed that I checked out library books
about girls I didn't see in school.

Now I hang the ornaments on the tree by myself.
My sister will come later,
maybe bringing record albums I'll treasure.
My brother sees no point in leaving California in winter.
He visited in fall and brought me a big pine cone,
about the size of a boot.

In front of the spangled tree, I look at my mother.
You never asked me what happened.

I know what happened, she replies.

You never ask how I'm doing.

I mind my own business, Mom says.
She lights a cigarette, tells me
that she and Dad plan to sell the house.
It's too big for two people and one dog.
She's sick of leaks that make the wallpaper peel.
The red linoleum in the kitchen, the green refrigerator.

I clean out my bureau drawers for the last time.
Sorting through papers, I find the letter Mom
asked Dad to give me in the Florida hospital.
She wrote: *I would have come,*
but I have a job interview this week.

She advised me to put this behind me
and included a short history lecture:
Just because White men did it to women
they kept on plantations doesn't make it right
for Black men to rape White girls now.
Hand flat as the side of a straw broom,
she shoved me back to an unfinished war.

I never said or wrote–Dear Mom:
Your timing was bad. But you were right
to look for places where past and present echo.
I was wrong to walk through a neighborhood

certain as Columbus of my right to be there,
wrong to be ignorant of history and politics.
And right to believe
a girl should be able to walk anywhere.

PART V

Paper Birds

At the Long Table

In Intro to Jazz Dance, we line up by the barre.
Our leg lifts are measured as they were in Ballet I,
though near the end of class,
our hips and shoulders may shimmy and shift.
I shower, change, then hurry across icy sidewalks.
On the first floor of the building
where English classes are taught,
long tables and chairs are set before wide windows.
Michael bends over a book across from Elizabeth,
who I know from a class where she often
raised her arm high, tilting her head
so her long, straight hair fell to one side.
A leather handbag with crisp folds sits by her elbow.

I wave as Michael beckons, but walk by mouthing, *Work.*
Does he like me? Do I like him?
Should I switch around the order of the questions?
My footsteps clang on the wide metal stairs.

As I slot mail into boxes
for the English professors, I chat with Jude,
who says Michael has been coming in a lot.
When I say I just saw him downstairs with Elizabeth,
she replies, *I don't think they're dating. He comes in here
and looks around, I think for you, then pours a cup of coffee.
The coffee at the student union is better.*

Maybe he's just fond of talking, like people I knew
in my first college. At UMass, most students rush off
after classes to jobs or activities. Michael doesn't have a job,
but he has a car, which kind of annoys me.
But is it foolish to believe I can't like anyone
who has more money than me? That's a wide field.

He's still at the long table when I come down
after my short shift, but now sits across from Deborah.
Her dark hair falls past silver hoop earrings.
Papers and poetry books sprawl before them.
I drape my black coat over a chair, tell them
I'm starting a fiction workshop with Professor Berg.
Michael says, *He seems kind of bitter.*

They all are, Deborah says. *I suppose they hoped
their books would become famous and they'd earn
enough money not to teach. Still, they insist
that the less popular the writing, the better it is.*

*Professor Berg seems better than the guy
who writes about fishing and hunting.
He thinks his acts are universal, but if women
write about making soup, it's just vegetables.*

I've gotten to know
professors who stop in the English office.
I pick up a book of Sylvia Plath's poems
among paperbacks scattered on the table.
They say "Ariel" is the first poem a woman wrote
about the conflict between motherhood and creativity.

It's not a conflict. Though yeah, it's easier
now that my daughter's in school, Deborah says.
But do we need a whole poem about it?
With one horrible word in the middle.

I put down the thin volume.
I'd like to read your take on motherhood.

I don't write about kitchens or playgrounds,
but do you want to exchange stories?
Deborah writes down her phone number, passes it to me.
She slips on a navy pea jacket and scoops up Frank O'Hara's
Lunch Poems.
I've got to pick up my daughter at school.

The Middle of an Eye

Michael and I watch Deborah's back as she hurries off.
Her tall, lean frame
makes her faded jeans look almost elegant.
Her boots are not the kind you'd wear to climb a mountain.
I ask, *Did you lend her that book?*

She'll give it back. Michael pauses.
She told me she did an independent study with Paul.
Some people say he favors girls.

He favors good writers. I don't mention the credits
Paul offered me for writing I did or didn't show him.
He writes fiction. You write poetry.

Not so much these days. The workload for teacher training
is heavy. He pauses again. *Are you really going*
to exchange writing with Deborah? She's kind of intense.

I think she's brave, I say. *To be a mother and to write.*

Michael lifts a shoulder, asks,
What awful word was she talking about?

I open *Ariel* to the title poem as if I knew.
But I'd forgotten gliding over the barbed word

used to describe the dark center of an eye.
I swallow. *She could have written* black.

It was a different time. Michael repeats
a standard line from English classes.

Not really. Sylvia Plath wasn't Mark Twain
showing life by the Mississippi River before the Civil War.
Sylvia wrote "Ariel" a hundred years later,
a time when bigots shouted at six-year-old Ruby Bridges.
I let myself skim the word
that surely stung or angered others.
I told myself Sylvia didn't mean to be cruel,
I don't mean to be cruel, but we are.

Sylvia lays blows against patriarchy,
but she also trades in stereotypes,
grabs imagery some claim she has no right to.
Writers should bend over each word,
consider the echoes, remember
that what we miss in the wide world matters.

The Fiction Workshop

Professor Berg's hair is the color of tarnished silver.
He has dark eyes, hunched shoulders, and a gravitas
he may have carried with him from Russia
or one of the nearby countries whose names change.
I read his collection of stories about people who worked
in Brooklyn shops that smelled of tobacco and old apples,
keeping silent about memories of mass murders
near fields where loved ones
once planted and dug potatoes.

We are twelve selected students, as if meant to be a jury,
though maybe it's just how many fit around a table.
We're told writers can be blind to our own words,
so while our stories are discussed, we must keep
our faces plain as plates, pretend the characters
only ever lived on paper, though most of us
write starting from life, then let words
blur, bend, and bridge toward their own truths.
Memory isn't enough. Art wants transformation.

The table is covered with papers
and canvas bags that wave like water.
Elizabeth's stiff handbag perches by her elbow.
She sits straight, often nodding at Professor Berg,
as if hoping to be mistaken for his assistant.

We read her good sentences about a girl and a horse.
There's not much to criticize, but little to love.

Ron's story is almost entirely dialogue,
troubled people talking about not very much.
We turn to one about a girl who scrapes
an almost entire cake into a trash can.
What's wrong with that girl? Ron asks.
Like, maybe she's not crazy but something else?
Anyway, it's too confessional.
He means: Don't be so revealing. Don't speak.

Divided Notebook

In my spiral notebook with five divided spaces,
I keep two sections for class notes,
another for drafts of stories or poems.
These sometimes spill into the sections
where I practice putting on paper
sentences I've only ever spoken to my therapist.
Memory appears without warning, like a ghost.
Rather than dodge or duck, I offer space
for what gets in the way of my efforts at fiction.

Every time I choose words, memory changes.
It's a storm. It's a wrecked beach. It's my life.

The Bottom of My Feet

I lift a blue-and-gold scrap of tapestry
off my typewriter, roll in a sheet of paper,
tap my fingers on the keyboard. I slip in
a narrow, sticky strip to white-over wrong words,
then punch in the right ones. Or good enough for now.
I think the class will hate this, but keep going
back to frost, knives, blood as my mother
reaches into the freezer, pulls out roast beef.
The color of the floor is burned into me,
the porcelain sink where I bathed dolls, flooded
a toy farm, rinsed seashells, and tie-dyed a shirt.

Memory isn't just an adversary, wrangling me down,
while I press back. On good days, memory nudges me
toward what's bigger than myself.
A cork bulletin board holds thumbtacked cards,
drawings, tests, and once a sheet with squares
where we glued the round tops of milk bottles
printed with presidents' faces.
This stopped when President Kennedy
was killed and the world changed.

At sixteen, I balanced on the radiator,
watching like a spy or maybe a writer
for what I should and shouldn't do to avoid

building my own prison, becoming my own walls.
In winter, heat spiraled and spit in shifts through the coils.
I leapt off when my socked soles started to burn.

Gifts

Dear Sylvia: You were eight when your father died.
Your mother then made a living teaching typing
and shorthand to girls training to be secretaries,
sweeping men's serious words into curlicues and waves,
then translating them at typewriters.
Your mother collected your excellent report cards,
pinned up notices of prizes.
When you offered news unworthy of boasting,
she said, *Pretend it was a dream.* Sylvia, I'm sorry.

Long ago our mothers were our houses.
They became shut doors. We don't tell them
what it's like to live with needles and scissors.
We write to the mothers we reached for,
haunted by what we weren't given, what we couldn't give.

Flutter

Paper birds strung on yarn hang from the ceiling.
Bright magnetic letters stick to the refrigerator.
Deborah glances at her daughter in a small room
off the kitchen. She bends over a puzzle
by a bureau with half-open drawers
overflowing with T-shirts, a stuffed elephant,
Where the Wild Things Are and *Beezus and Ramona.*

Deborah whispers, *Neil was supposed to watch*
Claire this weekend but there was some crisis.
At the co-op where he works? Playing saxophone?

Should I come back another time?
I don't know who Neil is, but I like that she assumes I do.

What if we just write instead of critiquing?
Deborah pushes aside electric and phone bills on the table.
She introduces me to her daughter,
who runs into the kitchen.

I want to write, too, Claire says. *I'll be quiet.*
Mommy, I know. You need quiet to think.
She puts a finger on her lips, then intently forms letters.
After a few minutes, she says, *People used to kill whales.*
That was mean. My teacher says I can write a story

about a whale but I have to spell it right.
There's a right way and a wrong way.
An e can be invisible. Not just eeeee.

Deborah aims narrowed eyes at her.
Claire finishes a page, lets it flutter to the floor.
She seems to write as if with no worry
of whether her words are good or bad.
The way I did when I was about her age, making
small books from arithmetic paper as soft as our hands.

Writing with a Goddess

Now I say, *I don't know where to start.*
Deborah taps *Lunch Poems.*
Michael told me that Frank O'Hara used to open a book
and put his finger on a word.
Then start from there. Or just look around.

A miniature photo that must be of Claire
as a newborn is propped by a plastic bear of honey.
An old, bent certificate with gold-winged angels
is pinned by a postcard of Picasso's *Guernica*
showing victims of war broken, patched,
twisted into animals, tears as big as boots.
Another postcard shows a thin woman holding
a staff as straight as her back. She balances a sun
between a headpiece with horns. I ask, *Who's that?*

The Egyptian goddess Isis, Deborah says.
Creator and destroyer. She had a child she raised alone.

I pick up my pen, write with almost
the confidence I had in the classroom
where I wrote hand-sized books. In second grade,
I sat in the last row, my back to pegs holding jackets.
In the front row the teacher placed boys known
to speak out of turn, stretch out a leg as an obstacle,
spit on scraps of paper they wadded up as weapons.

Our teacher steadied a yardstick
against the blackboard to make lines.
The script letters we practiced slanted like skaters.
Once, the yardstick slipped.
The teacher's chalk made a scrawl.
A boy laughed. Our teacher spun around,
raised the wooden yardstick the way Isis held up her staff.
The red-faced boy yanked back his hands.
The yardstick snapped on his desk,
as if splitting the world between good and bad.
The girls in the back believed
if we stayed quiet we'd be safe.

Sides

The following week I return to the kitchen
that smells of crayons and slightly burnt rice.
Food stamps are pitched on the table like unsteady tents.
Deborah and I slide each other copies of our stories.
We're instructed to start typing stories
down a third of a page, but hers begins
as close to the top as her typewriter allows.
I read about a sixteen-year-old girl
sitting beside a boy driving a fast car.
She listens to traffic, watches trees and houses blur,
wondering if and when she might tell
the boy she's pregnant. She savors the secret.

My story seems stupid in comparison.
The year I obsessed about my mother,
Deborah became one. *It's powerful,*
I say. *I want to know what happens to that girl.*

I started out writing poetry, but after Paul's class,
I focused on fiction, she says. *I want to turn*
these pages into a novel and maybe make some money.

I nod. Fiction commands bigger sections
of bookstores, with only one or two shelves of poetry,
where the living compete with the dead.
But my name on a cover seems a long way away.

On her bookshelf the spines of a few novels holding
scenes of feuds, arson, suicide
are as shiny as black licorice.
Deborah follows my gaze but reaches over books
by William Faulkner to pick up Allen Ginsberg's *Howl*.
Like *Lunch Poems*, the slim volume
is the size of a sandwich. She says,
It must have been great to write in New York in the 1950s.

Maybe if you were a guy, I reply.
Did any of the Beat poets ever do dishes?
Some seemed to live without much thought
for what was ahead or back to people left behind.
I like Frank O'Hara, but was he a Beat poet?
Any time you stick one word in front
of *poet* or *writer* you get something wrong.

When bankers were building skyscrapers,
the Beat poets said words mattered, not steel and glass.
They led truer lives than Sylvia Plath
with her pearls and fancy education.
I come from a town near the one
where she grew up, but not at all like it.

She wasn't wealthy, I say. *She got a scholarship.*

That's what I mean. She was always watched over,
Deborah says. *I don't feel sorry for her.*
She abandoned her children.

Surely Sylvia's pain was so deep
she couldn't see past it. Still, I can't defend that,
won't read about her last days.
Maybe I don't need her now that I'm becoming
friends with a living writer and mother.

If we met, Sylvia and I
probably wouldn't have liked each other.
With her waterfall of hair, curled under at the ends,
she would scorn my baggy black coat
and untended eyebrows, my silences
and stutter, the lines of my poems too long.
I wouldn't have just listened,
like we were coached to do at the hotline.
I would tell her, *Don't kill yourself.*
She'd probably call me naive.

Crossing

Wearing my favorite blue shirt and dangling earrings,
I run my fingers through my hair, which I washed last night,
though it still smells like the university pool.
Around the table the professor and eleven students
take out my story about a girl who crouches
on the radiator by a moss-colored refrigerator,
watching her mother dust
frost from a package of frozen beans,
jab a knife to see if blood still runs in the roast.
The mother never says, *I hurt,*
so the girl can't say it either.
Instead, she teeters on the radiator, plotting escape.

There are some good details. But does anything
happen? Ron asks. *I don't really like*
the narrator. I can't tell if she's sad or angry.

Maybe you don't have to tell, Elizabeth says.
She wears a sweater I think is cashmere: soft,
expensive, a pale pink without ink stains near the cuffs.
She says, *I see myself in this girl.*

The professor with hair the color of spoons says, *So do I.*

No Longer

Boxes of tea lined up on the stovetop have pictures
of a dragon, a wizard, a bear
wearing a red cap dozing on a soft green chair.
Deborah and I meet in her kitchen on Sunday
afternoons when Claire is with Neil. I've seen him
a few times at the door when they return.
His straight brown hair is pulled back in a ponytail.
I recognize him
from the register at the co-op, always friendly.
Deborah said she met him in community college
and he came along when she transferred here.
She told me he isn't Claire's father, but not who is.

I talk about her new story, another one
set almost entirely in a car. The driver seems a liar,
but maybe it's the narrator who's unreliable.
Deborah's sentences
are hard and plain as a wooden table.
I ask, *Is this the same sixteen-year-old girl who's pregnant?*

No! And this isn't about Neil. I just wanted
to put in a saxophone. Maybe I'll change it to drums.
She looks across the papers on the table at me.
I've been trying to break up with him
for over a year, but more seriously now.

He seems like a good guy. Offering an opinion
on a boyfriend or ex or something between
rarely ends well, but my words keep me from asking,
What about Claire? The two seem close.

He is a good guy. She shrugs. *After we moved here,*
he asked me to marry him. And adopt Claire.
That might have solved some problems but made more.
He hasn't made any connections to bands
here and you can't play saxophone solo.
He needs to be in a city where he can get gigs.

I'm not sure what she hopes for and I don't ask.
As we return to her story, I get up to boil water,
choose a tea bag from a box with a picture
of a tiger lounging amid huge flowers.

The Way the World Is

The spring day is unusually warm as I leave
a class. Some students read books while lying
on the grass or propping their backs against tree trunks.
I pass a brick building with a statue of a saint
holding out his arms above the glass doors.
A more modest building bears a six-pointed star.
Across an intersection, cans are balanced on porch
railings of sprawling fraternity houses.
All the boys have taken off their shirts,
as if making a pact to show their pale chests.
Two shout at me, scatter laughter like broken glass.

Just keep walking. Don't freak out.
I tell myself what I was coached to repeat,
what millions of women seem bound
to conclude: Don't make it a big deal.
That's just how the world is.
We're taught to never mind, never mind, never mind.

What Gleams

The room smells of freshly ground coffee.
I'm early to meet Deborah at a café
in a Victorian house with a wraparound porch.
Blueberry scones and chocolate cookies
are displayed under a clear dome.
I open my notebook by a wide china cup,
hear people passing offices and a shop selling
earrings and necklaces made with semiprecious stones.

I write a lot of bad lines on the way to writing a good one.
That's just how it goes, shifting confidence and doubt.
I bend over my notebook like the jeweler,
his long hair tucked behind his ears.
He holds a magnifying glass, wields a cloth
to make what's no longer rough gleam.

Oh, here she is, saying,
There was a long line at the copy shop.
Deborah hands me a slightly warm stack of papers.
What are you writing? begins our conversations.
Her story is another about a couple
who aren't really a couple. Silence deepens
between their spoken words, like the low parts
of waves before they curl up and break.
It's another story with no child.

Does she write around a baby, the way I circle rape?
I wonder if any of these guys is like Claire's father,
but I don't ask, not wanting to seem nosy
as the villagers who judged Hester Prynne.

The dialogue is sharp, I say. *So good.*
I say more complimentary, true things before
pointing out a few words that don't seem to belong.

Mistakes make a work come alive.
Deborah braces her back. She's not a fan of criticism.
I mean, who is? She asks, *What did you write?*

I shrug. There's little use in showing someone work
when I already recognize lines I can't get away with.
It wasn't good enough yet.

They never are, Deborah says.
*Maybe you try too hard. Allen Ginsberg's motto
was: "First thought, best thought."*

Maybe that worked for him. Or he made it up.
It sounds cooler than revising all the time.
Still, a jeweler can polish too much
and be left with dust. A reach for perfection
can be as dangerous as a broken edge of glass.

The Umbrella

It's the middle of Professor Berg's office hours
when I arrive, but he's putting on his worn raincoat.
His desk is mostly clear
but for a framed photograph of Tolstoy,
his gray, wrinkled hair and beard spread to his chest.
Shelves are packed with books.
I read one of the two books with his name on the cover,
the same number that Sylvia published before she died.

The professor picks up a black umbrella,
talking as we leave the building.
Students skirt puddles by a grand tree,
a smaller, blooming, soggy magnolia.
Bells peal from the old stone chapel.
He says, *I don't know if I should say this.*
But you can be a writer. He laughs
as he adds, *It could ruin your life.*

The moment in light rain is not as gleaming
as the prizes and awards Sylvia collected,
but the words imprint a memory
of the chapel's gray stone,
the ducks' brown-and-green feathers,
raindrops stamping small circles on the pond.
Water rippled before the professor opened
his umbrella, but I hadn't seen.

Chalk

Deborah, Claire, and I sometimes swim in a pond
across from a dam where the reckless jump.
We go to a park
where we fry eggs and make toast on a grill.
Now that school is out, Claire is mostly around,
so Deborah doesn't report on conversations with Neil.
I have nothing to say about Michael,
who's again gone for most of the summer,
traveling in England with his father to
see more Shakespeare.

One afternoon we walk into town.
Claire inspects the grass for insects.
Sometimes she seems younger than seven,
skipping over cracks in the sidewalk,
and sometimes older, checking the time,
anxious about being where she should be.

In the library we're told Deborah
didn't pay the fine for a missing book.
Her hands clench. Her cheeks slightly puff.
I might have said something, but Claire
is already backing away. Outside the door,
empty-handed, she says, *She was mean.*

She wasn't mean, Deborah says. *They have rules.*
We need to look for that book.

We don't like rules, do we, Mom? Claire says.

We stop in the ice cream shop, coo at a baby
wearing a violet sweater with buttons
the size of her two glossy, tiny teeth.
An older sister stamps a soft, sandaled foot.

The jeweler, now wearing his long hair loose,
smiles at Deborah as if he sees a past or future.
Her gaze slides over and past him.
When we leave, she tells me, *Some guys*
like the picture Claire and I make together,
but they don't see themselves in the frame.

On her street, people type by open windows.
Claire stops to play at the corner house
by theirs, with a sign for shoe repair.
Children write their names
on the driveway with colored chalk.
A small girl drawing chalk circles around herself
reminds me of the toddler I cared for as a mother's helper.

I tell Deborah about how she lay on her back
and rolled, hugging a bag of marshmallows.

Do you want to have children? Deborah asks.

I'm not in a relationship, I say before remembering
she became a mother with no guy
in the picture and a writer, too.
I like kids, but there's a lot to figure out.

*Being pregnant then a mother taught me
how much you can't control,* she says.

Under September Boughs

I tape up flyers announcing that Maya Angelou
will read next Wednesday at four
here in the English Department building.
Heading down the stairs, I see Michael coming up.
We stop at the place where the wide stairs turn,
the best place for posters, and I point to one.
Maya Angelou! I take a breath. *Will you go?*

He looks past my shoulder, shrugs. *It's not a great time.*

I nod, hurt, then embarrassed. Did he think
I was asking him on a date? Was I?
I wave toward the bottom of the stairs.
I'm on my way to my other job.

He offers to join me, walking past the Newman Center,
Hillel, sprawling houses marked with Greek letters.
Michael talks about the courses
he's taking to teach high school English.
I ask, *Are you writing any poems?*
When he says he's been busy, I ask,
Will you have enough poems to apply to grad school?

I'm going straight to teaching.
There are more ways than writing to open doors.

I don't want to think that writing and teaching
must be separate. I just signed up for
some teacher training courses. Before I can say this,
Michael stops under long leafy branches.
Remember when I told you Clark
offered to critique my poems? he asks.
He invited me to go over them at a cabin
he built just for writing back when his kids were young.

As he pauses the whoosh and grind
of passing cars seem to stop.
Light ripples through leaves above us.
It wasn't my poems he was interested in.

My breath catches with a click.
I'm sorry. That's horrible.
I should have known. Did I know?

Michael's mouth wobbles.
His shoulders are slumped, his voice thick.
I know this happens more to women.

I should say no one has to measure pain,
but I blurt out, *You can't stop writing!*

His mouth sags like a disappointed teacher.

He says goodbye and turns to walk back to his car.

The bottom of his jacket splits into a *V*,

widening, then closing again.

Michael doesn't say, as Rachel did,

that he was stupid to accept the invitation.

Still, he stopped writing poetry. This is how a story ends.

PART VI

Breaking Light

Masks

Maya Angelou could command a large stage,
but that September afternoon she stands in front
of a room of about thirty professors and a few students.
Professor Clark, whose hair is the color
of shadowed snow, introduces her as an old friend.
I don't remember whether she wore a turquoise gown
or red-and-purple shawl, but billowy cloth was bright
as the patterned scarf wound around her head.

As she speaks, her hands wave their own song.
A woman who was raped as a girl,
commanded not to tell, now sings, sways,
laughs, and writes whatever she wants.

After reading "Phenomenal Woman,"
Maya recites from memory a poem
by Shakespeare, then one by Edgar Allan Poe,
another by Paul Laurence Dunbar,
who long ago wrote of why caged birds sing.
Reciting his "We Wear the Mask," Maya twists
her face but keeps her eyes on Professor Clark
seated by his wife, mother to their grown children.
His smile is stiff, as if to ward off her look
that's knowing, unflinching, and offering grace.
Michael should be here. Who else like him
may sit on one of the folding metal chairs?

No Previews

Deborah and I plan to go to a movie
after Neil picks up Claire for the weekend.
But when I reach their apartment, Claire says hello,
then bends close to her drawing.
Deborah clangs dishes too hard in the sink.
When Neil comes in, Claire jumps into his arms.
Deborah gives him a burning look. *You're late.*
We missed the beginning of the movie.

I didn't know you were going to a movie.
Neil's voice is even. He nods hello to me,
then asks Claire, *Did you pack your bag?*
She grins and holds up her ladybug-printed backpack.

We won't go now. We missed the beginning!
Deborah wipes an arm over the refrigerator.
Bright magnetic letters clatter to the floor.

There are previews. I ache to pick up *B, Z, P, C,*
but hold my arms still. *Anyway, we can*
get something to eat. Really, I'd rather just talk.

As Neil and Claire leave, Deborah leads
me to the living room, plunks on the sofa
she unfolds each night to sleep on.

I'm sorry to miss that movie.
Claire says the three of us should all live
together like normal people, Deborah says.
That's over. I have to stop seeing him even at the door.

I could say, *You can always call me.*
I worry for Claire. But I've got two jobs,
a full load of classes, therapy I'm struggling
to cut back on, and writing. I say, *You're strong.*

I hate when people say that.
Deborah's face flushes. *It's like they refuse*
to see everything I missed to become who I am.

Of course. What we couldn't do becomes part of us.
Everyone has stories that take years, not minutes, to tell.
While rocks are battered by waves,
sand ever so slowly, beautifully crumbles.

Sorry

My old fiction professor, an editor at the university
literary magazine, helped arrange a work-study job there.
I'll no longer tape up posters
and sort mail in the English office.
In the *Review*'s smoky basement room, I take directions
from a woman who's fine using the word *secretary*.
At a desk pushed against hers, I slit envelopes,
slip out stories or poems I sort and catalog for the editors.

The idea of certain greatness I carried
from lit classes crumbles as manuscripts
waved high by one editor are sneered at by another.
After some fierce but failed defenses, I insert
a manuscript back into a self-addressed envelope
along with a printed card noting regret.
Part of my job is signing
this cream-colored card with *Sorry*.
A bit of handwriting apparently eases the sting.

I write *Sorry* over and over to have a stack at the ready.
It's like a mantra with an undertone of
Nothing personal. Try again.

Looking Ahead

Balls of crumpled paper lie on the floor
like balloons fallen after a party.
Deborah points to these when I ask what she's been writing.
I'll wait to show her my work.
I don't talk about my job at the *Review*, which even
after a few weeks I think may be the best job I'll ever have.
My work is mundane, but I like listening to conversations
in the manuscript-and-magazine-packed office.
I don't say much
about my class studying lost women writers,
where I'm learning my way around interlibrary loans
and archives to find hidden pasts and my possible future.
I tell her I started teacher training courses.

Teaching? Oh my God, no, she cries.
What about your writing? You can be great!

The stationery store is okay, but I don't want
to be one of the people who works there forever.

You'll sell a book!

If I'm lucky. Even at my most hopeful,
I believe that will take years.
I guess I can write on weekends and summers.

What teacher really does that?
I have to meet with a social worker
to get money for being in college.
It's supposed to lead somewhere.
She wants me to be like her or a teacher.
Someone who thinks she knows better than anyone else,
who'd never have gotten pregnant at sixteen.

Maybe we can be a new kind of teacher.
But I can't really see Deborah with her hair pulled back,
coaxing students through *Tess of the d'Urbervilles*.
I'm not sure about me. Can I grade
stacks of papers about whether fault lies more
with an individual or society? Could I bear
to hear students examine the moment,
though off the page,
when a girl assesses her flagging strength and considers
whether everything might hurt less if she stops resisting?
I was one of those girls who shifted hope for help
to hope to live, decided defeat offered
the best chance to see the sky another morning.

Outsiders examine the caliber of a rapist's threats,
decide how much sympathy a girl deserves.

Like with the women called witches
who drowned when dunked, the only proof
she fought hard enough is if she's dead.

Lost and Found

Sixteen serious girls squeeze into a seminar room,
drape coats over chairs, let books spill from knapsacks.
We each choose to study diaries, letters, and notes
of a little-known woman writer,
including a missionary, farmer, botanist,
a leader in a small, mostly Black church.
I discover a novelist who wrote in the days
of horses and buggies, when a girl could grow up
seven miles from the ocean and never see the waves.
All of us find what we believed did not exist.

One girl focuses on a nineteenth-century widow
who supported five children by editing a magazine.
She also wrote most of what was printed inside,
likely including the poem about Mary and her lamb.
I want to be on the side of my hometown,
but it seems likelier the poem was composed
by Sarah Josepha Hale, who wrote about fifty books,
than by a fellow said to have passed through our town,
then never published another word.
Uncertainty opens a way forward.
It can't be set in marble,
like a small statue of a lamb, but is beautiful, too.

Places We Don't See

Deborah puts on a favorite record:
Duke Ellington playing "Take the 'A' Train."
The postcards of Isis, ruler over life and death,
sky as well as earth, and Guernica
are on her kitchen table. She's trying to rescue
them from splattered spaghetti sauce.

I ask about what she's writing,
but Deborah changes the subject.
The social worker keeps grilling me
about what I'll do after graduation.
She doesn't understand a writer
has to be ready when inspiration comes.
She picks up the postcard of Guernica, rubs a red splatter.
I always wanted to see this painting.

It takes up most of a wall. Last spring I took
a bus sponsored by the Art History Department
on a day trip to New York. I went to museums
and saw my old housemate. Rachel showed me
the small theater where she works in a cramped office.
She wore a black shirt and jeans,
like all the backstage crew, though
I don't think she works in lighting anymore.

I want to go to New York. And Paris. And Santa Fe,
Deborah says. *What am I talking about?*
I'll never go anywhere. I'm so tired. Did I say that?
I got myself into this. Everyone says so.
Pregnant at sixteen. I don't regret it.
She turns to the tiny picture of Claire as a baby.
The round face, the shock of dark hair,
the soft, raised fists. *I miss those days.*
It was hard, never getting much sleep,
but I loved holding a life in my arms.

The lines by Deborah's mouth are taut as a clothesline.
She puts her head on the table, wraps her arms
around it, then opens them to look at me.
It was impossible to keep seeing Neil,
but it's hard not to ever get a break from mothering.
What I'd really like is one morning
when I can get out of bed whenever I want.

Your Sweater's Inside Out

Claire scans the big books
on a bottom shelf in my bedroom.
She settles on the yellow-gold book of myths
I brought from the place I still call home.
After I read a few, Claire wants
to write a story, then read it to me.
We stay up too late, before she settles on
a sleeping bag on the floor.
When I wake her up, her first words are *I'm tired.*

It's not even light out and already I'm failing.
I wonder if I should cook eggs, decide cereal is fine,
though Claire announces
it's not the kind her mother buys.
She gets dressed, then spins around the kitchen.
Mom says I can take ballet classes.

Those girls are strong. Noncommittal. I don't want
to suggest she should or shouldn't count on lessons.
I beckon her over and carefully unsnarl her soft hair.

My mom just pulls the comb through.
Claire's voice is solemn.
She says it hurts, but it's over sooner.

I don't use more force. I snap in a barrette.

Claire steps out from between my legs.

The striped pattern of her sweater is blurred.

A pinched line of stitching marks the tops of the sleeves.

I say, *Your sweater is inside out.*

Claire glares. *My mother lets me wear it like this.*

Plain

Claire's eyes are fierce as mine must have been
when I was her age and stood on the church steps
listening to ladies praise my father for carrying on
while my mother was sick. Some called him a saint.
One asked me, *What's his favorite dessert?*
I wouldn't say pie or cake, something flaky or chocolate.
I told her, *Jell-O,* which she later presented
with slivers of cherries bright as lipstick,
suspended grapes, and pale sliced pears caught within.

When I brought back the washed bowl,
the neighbor asked if there was anything else
she could do, maybe use different fruit next time?
I said, *We like it plain.* I didn't want anyone to think
we needed what our mother couldn't or wouldn't make.

Long ago my voice was steady,
loyal to mothers or love.
That child is gone. Or maybe not.
Can I listen to all the girls I've ever been?
The second grader who wrote small books
that opened like safety pins or wings.
The girl who pulled her friend from a car
when she sensed danger.
The girl who failed to rescue another friend

from a man in a shop who sat by a tub
of bobbing soda bottles and said, *Help yourself.*

Can I forgive her and the girl who walked
into a neighborhood that wasn't hers?
What if instead of hating them for heading
toward trouble, I sat with an open basket?
The girls I blamed are the girls who saved me, too.

Measuring

Waiting at a coffee shop, I overhear talk
about President Nixon's resignation in disgrace,
the recent Vietnam War, and the Trojan War.
A bearded man clips words from discarded copies
of classroom handouts. A melon-sized mound rises.
Maybe he plans to turn these into a poem.

When Michael arrives, instead of spilling
poetry books from his knapsack,
he shows me novels written for teens.
The school where I practice teach won't buy these.
They blame budgets, but some mistrust books
they weren't raised on. All written for adults,
by men, a long time ago. He talks about
The Scarlet Letter, Moby Dick, and *Walden,*
tells me one of his classes is reading Anne Frank's diary.
Some say it's a good way to introduce the Holocaust.
But her line about people being basically good drives me nuts.
Nazis wanted to kill her and her family.

Anne Frank knew more than what she wrote.

I guess that's true for a lot of people.

Michael, I'm sorry for . . ., I blurt out. *When you told me*
about your poetry professor and his stupid cabin,
I was wrong to say: You have to write.

Someone had to say that, he replies.
If I ever write poems again, it may be because of you.
But I was never going to be someone
like Emily Dickinson or Frank O'Hara.

I probably won't be great either, but I like to write.
At least when it's not making me feel crazy.

Anyway, that was a long time ago, he says.
A lot of people deal with worse.

Everything matters. Can't we just say that?
But I'm quiet as Michael takes out a hand-drawn map
with two straight lines veering out, a dot between.
A friend made this to show where Emily Dickinson
was buried. I'm traveling with my father
over January break, but maybe
we could go when I get back. And it's warmer.

House by the Woods

Logs crackle and hiss. I sit by a fireplace
and a dozing dog named after a fairy
in Shakespeare. Making my way toward a poem,
every line is a chance to embarrass myself.
I write lots of sentences not worth saving.
That will never change.
But on a good day, what I want to know
and don't want to know come together in words.

An editor at the *Review* asked me to stay
in his old house on the edge of the woods
while he and his wife travel between semesters.
It's the first Christmas I don't spend with my parents.
It's like a writing retreat in exchange
for watching the dog and making sure the old furnace
doesn't quit, or if it does, calling the number
he left of another English professor who knows what to do.
I was free to use their car and told I could set
the electric blanket to any temperature I please,
but the dog prefers her side on medium.

After supper, I wash a warped wooden plate.
I open my notebook, peel an orange,
put the scent in a sentence. I start from life,
then follow words that surprise me

into what I didn't know I knew.
I'm doing exactly what I want to be doing
even as I feel alone with a story
that stops like a crack in the earth
where a girl or a goddess might tumble.
Maybe the absence of an ending
lets me enter my story where I choose.

Wooden Tiles

On an icy sidewalk outside the ice cream shop,
I run into the old high school friend
who slipped me notes decorated with stars.
We shared oranges at lunchtime.
She introduces me to a big-smiling guy
who works with her in a clinic for hurt animals.
I'm glad she's alive and no longer living
in a high-rise dorm with the boyfriend I didn't like.

We arrange to meet at her home and talk more.
Afterward, I begin a story about someone
like me who drives a borrowed car through
a snowstorm down twisting back roads.
Late at night, over a Scrabble board, my friend confides
that her old boyfriend used to hit her.
I tell her some of what can be said only
between two girls who found a way back
to each other by a loom, a wood stove,
and curtains drawn over snowy windows.

Edges

My throat is sore as if I swallowed sand
while Deborah reads my not-yet-finished story.
After she puts down the pages, I tell her
more of what's behind the friends' broken dialogue.
I limit description, not wanting to put too much
on someone with problems of her own, or do I mean me?
Deborah says, *Rape must be hard to write about.*

Yes, but also hard to not write about.
Memory pulls me like Persephone
who has no choice but to return again and again.
Maybe she became stronger
each time she crossed between worlds.

Not Dancing

I don't need to tell everything to everyone or anyone
but I need the courage and hope to know I can.
These days I can change the subject as quickly
as Persephone dusted off her feet when back above ground.

I pick up Deborah's story about a doomed couple,
a girl filled with yearning,
another guy who wants to be somewhere else.
I praise the way their conversation
pitches like the ocean waves they walk by.
If you want this to be part of a novel,
maybe the girl should be more consistent? I suggest.

Deborah shrugs, puts the paper away.
She tells me about a new friend who's a mom
who offered to share a babysitter when they go
to a barn converted to a dance hall. *A good band*
is playing on Saturday. Want to come?

I shake my head. I went to this place with her once.
I didn't like the way she turned her head,
flicked her hand when guys she didn't want
to dance with approached. Or the way
I talked to some, which wasn't kinder.
I hated shouting over loud music to be heard.

Now that Neil and I are over, I need to get out more,
she says. *My friend offered to introduce me to someone*
who's graduating this spring from the business school.
He's already lined up a job with a big firm in Chicago.

I guess my eyebrows go up, because she adds,
I know. He doesn't sound like my type.
That's what I told her, but she said:
Where have those musicians and poets gotten you?

Starting with One Word

I slide my story into my canvas bag.
I mean to revise it in response to the word
violence we were given as a writing prompt
in a class for teaching writing in high school.
We're supposed to do exercises we'll later offer students.
The instructor favors words like *pedagogy* and *heuristics*,
which make me and my best friend in class, a poet, wince.
Didn't he remember: *No ideas but in things?*
Or E. B. White's advice to prefer
the concrete to the abstract?

The word *violence* is vague enough to muffle
the sound of screams, the sharp point of scissors on skin,
the sting in a scalp as a handful of hair is loosened.
It's a request to reply with other dignified abstractions.
Instead, I offer the clicking of Scrabble tiles,
the scent of lemon in tea, a loom
laced with yarn and feathers,
the ragged turns in conversation,
close then and away from memory and its blades.

The professor returns my piece with polite margin notes.
He doesn't act offended as I hoped he'd be:
I was mad that he seemed not
to consider that even a bloated word
might touch the real throat of a real person.

If I ever get a job in a high school,
I vow to never ask anyone to write
about violence expecting they never knew it.

Hands

Danger: Thin Ice signs surround
the campus pond where I meet Michael.
He takes out the hand-drawn map
we try to follow in his car to a cemetery.
Walking side by side, almost but not quite touching,
we read gravestones as if from a bookshelf
where we recognize no names. He tells me
about Irishmen who worked in the Dickinson yard
and stables, then carried Emily's casket.
Her best friend, Sue, made sure
her grave was lined with pine boughs.

After giving up on finding the poet's name,
Michael and I stand by a picket fence,
listening to the traffic
as if someone might stop and point out where to look.
His fingertips on my wrist become a hand
on the small of my back, which I like.

I slip off my gloves, take his hand.
Our palms are warm together.
He looks into my eyes, then asks,
May I kiss you? His lips are warm.

Unreadable

Maybe everything would have been different
if our first kiss hadn't happened in a cemetery.
Or if we'd found what we were looking for.
But over the next weeks, I find that wanting
to be in love isn't the same as being in love.
One night I broil eggplant,
sprinkle cinnamon into the tomato sauce.
One morning he makes pancakes,
too raw in the middle.
He says, *Really, teaching isn't easy. I was naive*
to think if I liked the students, they'd like me.

I can't write in the room where he grades papers.
I pick a few fights.
I hate a poster on his bedroom wall.
How can he not like dogs?
One Saturday he wants to hike together
and I say I need time alone to write.
He suggests I'm testing him. Maybe.

Still, when Michael says,
I don't think this will work out, I cry.
He gives me the map
to the cemetery we couldn't read.
I tape it to my wall, like a small piece
of abstract art, cryptic as Emily's poems.

Bonfire

Is there something wrong with me?
Anger comes in bewildering ways.
I am a novice at tenderness.
I've heard plenty of warnings
about how a life like mine can be wrecked.

Dear Sylvia: Am I meant to be lonely?
You might say I should be bolder, look wider,
but if we're going to be honest,
there's not one guy in *The Bell Jar*
I'd care to know, even those who didn't ask
a girl to tango and tore off half her dress.
You dated and cast off many before dancing
with the man with a lock of dark hair falling over one eye,
who wrote poems about hunting and crows.
You said your marriage four months later was fated.

I don't believe in fate. And I don't much like Ted,
though the letters you wrote in the next few years
read like a romance. When the two of you traveled,
you brought watercolors to sketch lakes and sky.
You taught at Smith, while he taught at UMass.
The two of you made a Ouija board by cutting
letters from magazines, pasting them in an arc
on a board, penning *Yes* and *No* at either end.
You wanted divine inspiration

for the poetry you wrote on the same sofa,
sometimes leaning against each other's backs.

After moving from Massachusetts to England,
you borrowed money to buy an old house in the country.
You wrote in a room with a view
of an apple orchard, old slate headstones.
You gave birth to a girl then a boy,
painted hearts on a cradle, crushed berries to make jam.
In spring, the hills turned yellow with daffodils.
You sold bunches at the village market.
You sewed red corduroy curtains, planted roses,
set up beehives, collected honey you stored in glass jars.

But even before a turn in the arc of a tale,
babies wailed, bees stung,
thorns pricked when you cut roses.
After leaves turned brown and fell,
darkness came early on fog or rain.
Watch out. I wish I could save you.
You layered on sweaters, avoided washing your hair
that never seemed to dry in the damp and chill.
You longed for a camel hair coat
and complained about not having a refrigerator.
Ted called you a spoiled American.

I imagine your cold hands as you picked up
the phone, listened to him talk on another upstairs.
You recognized the woman's whisper,
ripped the phone from the wall.

Fierce as Isis, whose picture you hung
over your daughter's crib, you smashed
a wooden table. In the backyard you lit a torch,
made a bonfire of some of Ted's poems and papers
and yours. Stop. Don't tell me more.
If I get too close to the end of your story,
will you leave me? Or will I leave you?

Cold Coffee

Deborah and I plan to meet in the university coffee shop.
A man dressed entirely in red
bends over a notebook filled with minuscule script.
I overhear a boy ask another, *What would it be like*
if Copernicus hadn't been born? His friend says,
I guess someone else would have figured out
we're not at the center of the universe.
The teacher of my old jazz dance class,
a striking Black man, is surrounded by thin White
girls with straight backs holding Styrofoam cups.
His intro class was popular even though
we met at eight in the morning.

Deborah hurries in, apologizes for being late.
She gives me one and a half pages.
Her sentences are taut as an anchored rope.
I say, *Maybe you could turn it into a poem.*

She folds the story, puts it away.
Is writing worth it? How do you know when to quit?

I catch my breath at a question I never had.
Write just a few more pages and you can send it out.
I could make you a list with addresses
of magazines who might like yours.

You don't know what it's like to be a single mom.
No one can do this alone. Not even your Sylvia Plath.
Raising a kid is hard. But you don't abandon them.

That's not the whole story. It's not even the end.
Sylvia was depressed. A lot of treatments didn't work
for her. She didn't really have a choice.

Jeannine, everyone has choices. She was selfish.

I watch the dance teacher stand, nod at the girls,
and leave, his beautiful back erect.
The girls buy brownies to split. They slump now,
putting their feet on chairs or one another's laps.
I remember stretching at the barre while our teacher
watched the long hand of the clock rise to twelve,
then shut the wide doors, snapped the lock.
No latecomer would come through those doors.
He spun around and reminded us
that if we ever took a class in a big city studio,
there'd be no forgiveness. He wanted us to be ready.

Close

Boot tracks are stamped in snowmelt on the library floor.
I kneel on my black coat to be close to low shelves,
slip out books, grateful even for those I swiftly slide back.
I find an article about Sylvia Plath by someone
who claims he was her friend during her last days.
Maybe. It seems Sylvia left batches of letters,
diaries, perhaps even an unpublished novel or two.
Much is in the care of the husband who left her
for another woman and burned at least one diary,
her last one, and lost some of her writing.
Ted Hughes claimed he meant to protect their children,
ensure her legacy
and his. He told their literary friends,
She's crazy. Don't believe her.

After he left the house with the beehives and roses,
Sylvia packed bedding, the soft, stitched lamb,
the little red hood she sewed for her daughter,
baby bottles, jars of applesauce.
What does it take to tether oneself to the world?
A burlap sack of potatoes, six jars of honey,
the voice of a toddler singing about the alphabet,
a baby just learning to say, *Mama, no,* and *light.*

How I Became a Bird

My black coat swishes against my jeans.
I stayed too long in the library,
am surprised by darkness. The leaning fence
meant to keep people safe from falling bricks
seems permanent though weather battered,
just sturdy enough to keep in docile farm animals.
I pass the pond, the old stone chapel, an intersection.
Shattered glass glints in car lights by a smudge of feathers.

By sprawling houses with Greek letters,
a boy shouts from a porch. He sets down a can,
throws one leg then the other over a railing.
He crosses frozen grass toward me.

He's a drunk frat boy, probably not dangerous,
but every such calculation I ever made
collapses to scrape up a scream
that started years ago, now rising on rage.
I claim tears instead of fighting them.
I throw out my arms,
then flap them.
I leap and spin,
my coat whirling
fast as a blackbird strewing feathers and flight.

I hear the boy mutter, *She's crazy*.
I keep spinning until I'm dizzy.
I drop my spread arms then raise them
high toward the beautiful, dark sky.
This time let the boy disappear, not me.

Becoming

A postcard of the mountain Cézanne painted
over and over, as if it moved during the night,
is propped against a blue clay mug filled with pens.
Writing isn't just finding language to set scenes
but erasing words that block what can be discovered
when two moments stand side by side.

I keep typing until I start to feel tender
toward what's under my hands.
I'm writing my way back into a black coat,
then may unstitch, like a bird losing feathers.
Slowly, I am writing my own home.

Beyond My Wooden Table

I thumb through literary magazines stacked
in the *Review* office, write lists of editors' names.
I address envelopes, tuck stories inside.
In the post office a worker weighs my manuscripts
on a small scale. He sells me the necessary stamps
should my enclosed envelope be returned.
Most are, so it seems as if I'm sending letters to myself.
The rejections sting. I send out another story the next day.
Try to return to the cocoon of nobody looking,
quietly reaching for something that shines first for me.

In Sylvia's last year of high school, after forty-five rejections,
she published a story in *Seventeen* magazine.
In all her years ahead she often read lines like:
I'm afraid this does not suit our needs. Sorry.
Sylvia cried, seethed, and sent her work elsewhere.
Isn't that hope?

Sylvia wrote despite rejections,
despite success, despite illnesses,
despite her mother's pressure.
She wrote she wrote she wrote she wrote well.
Ambition hurled like a rock through her life.
Maybe she wanted too much, but is that a crime?
Like the person I'm trying to become,
she stood by her writing.

Burnt

The kitchen smells like used matches.
I spent the afternoon making a supper no one wanted,
Deborah says. *Then wrecked the chocolate chip cookies.*
They sprawl into each other
on a baking sheet left on the stove.
Claire says hello, but hunkers with her back near the wall.
Her eyes dart like a small animal amid traffic.
My voice is low, tentative: *Did I come at a bad time?*

We were having a discussion. Deborah's voice is tight.
Claire keeps asking to see Neil.

Mommy, I miss him.

I told you, no. Deborah raises an arm
as if reaching for sky, but she's not. Her arm falls.
Claire twists her small body against the wall
where the postcards of Isis and *Guernica* are taped.
Claire tucks in her head, freezes in place,
then rushes to her room.

Deborah wipes her wrist across her face,
bends over to breathe. Her wavy hair grazes
her knees before she straightens. *I'm so tired.*
She says more about that, but I'm not listening.
Don't yell at her, I say. *Don't . . .*

Deborah nods. Our eyes lock in a vow.
She says, *I started dating the guy*
in business school my friend told me about.
I like him. But it's hard for Claire.

Of course it's hard. I study the sprawling cookies.
Where's your spatula? The tops look okay.

While Deborah goes to Claire's room,
I start scraping off the black bottoms.
It's impossible to remove every burnt crumb,
which will ruin the taste of the rest.
I push the cookies deep into the trash
and scrub the blackened pan.

Deborah returns to the kitchen,
tells me Claire is reading.
I want to see her, but Deborah and I settle
in the other room where she says,
Really, I'll be a better mother.
I promise. That's all that matters, isn't it?

The Torn-Down Door

Just after dawn, boxes of donuts are passed around
the art bus. Also, copies of a hand-drawn map
marked with museums, galleries,
and the drop-off and pick-up spots.
Deborah wants to see what people call art now
rather than years ago, so after arriving in New York,
we visit a few galleries. Some art
is made of cement and ropes, variously knotted,
or collages of torn letters and photographs.
Clay trees with bare branches seem to stop nowhere.
One wall is empty with just a small card
with the name of the work and artist.

In Greenwich Village–is it pretentious to say the Village?
Deborah recognizes the name of a tavern.
Frank O'Hara wrote poems on napkins here.
Does that mean she intends to write?
We go inside, order sandwiches. I jot down
some words on a napkin, then push it away.
Were the napkins once bigger, the light better?

A man with brown-and-gray hair wearing
a corduroy jacket comes over, introduces himself.
He tilts his head toward the bathroom.
Jack Kerouac tore down that door.

He stood on the bar to read from On the Road.
He didn't need a fancy podium or stage.
Beat poets read from ladders, like workmen,
or in cafeterias or on abandoned piers.
He asks our names. Deborah says she's a poet.

Me too, he says. *I published one book, but no one*
will take another since it didn't make money.
That's all publishers care about.

A writer doesn't need to rip down doors
or stand on a bar. I turn to Deborah.
We should go. You wanted to see Guernica.

The painting? the man asks. *That's in Spain.*

I saw it in the Museum of Modern Art, I reply,
though now I'm wondering if I can trust
my memory. And are you supposed to say MoMA?
I don't know how that's pronounced.

You must have confused it with something else by Picasso.
The man nods toward the front door. *In the 1950s,*
typewriters sat on tables outside of bookshops here.
People could just stop and write whatever came
into their minds. What poets do you like?

Deborah mentions several Beat poets.
When I'm silent, she says, *She likes Sylvia Plath.*
A dry laugh funnels up through her.

Yes. Yes, I do. *She wasn't selfish.*
But I'm afraid Deborah's right, and that
if I read more about and imagine Sylvia's last days
I won't like the woman who's long kept me company.
I stand and ask, *Are you coming?*

Deborah shakes her head. *I want to stay.*

I follow the lines on the hand-drawn map.
In the museum, I look at the breaking horse and bull,
pieces of howling people, patches of newsprint
not quite holding everything together.
I was right that *Guernica* was here, but does it matter?
I find one of Cézanne's shifting mountains,
collapsing what was, making room for the new.
When do artists turn from what's before
their eyes to make something new?
I like the blue, yellow, and pink ponds of Monet.
Water spreads but doesn't splinter light.

On Our Way Home

Deborah is one of the last people to step on the bus.
She looks around without catching my eye, pauses,
then silently sits beside me, her back straight.
Around us people's voices rise, excited,
as the bus pulls into the street.
Paper rustles as some open magazines, unwrap food.

Everyone gets quieter as we leave the city lights.
By the time we cross into Connecticut there's a sleepy hush.
Deborah says, *I can't believe you left me.*
I almost didn't get here in time.
And they said, forget about it if you're late.

You had a map.

I didn't take one. I thought I'd be with you.

Guernica *was in the museum.*
I forgot how big it is, so powerful.

Don't tell me about it.
Backs of necks stiffen as if people
in front of us are trying not to turn them.
I face the window. Lights streak in our wake,
blur and shine like the ponds I saw on the walls.

Everything is hard, Deborah says.
Sometimes I thought about killing myself.
I watch fast cars and trucks head the other way.
I forget who first reached, but Deborah and I
hold hands like children, old ladies, or maybe
two friends getting ready to say goodbye.
I say, *I used to think about suicide, too.*

Maybe it wasn't just Claire who kept me here,
Deborah says. *We don't really know, do we?*

It rains or it stops raining and a girl
puts down scissors, a bottle of pills.
Someone says hello on the street
and a girl walks away from a bridge over a river.
No one knows what makes someone keep on.
Or another person swallow
needles and pins, open an oven door.
Somewhere a phone rings and no one answers.

Clear Walls

Sylvia pushed a pram holding her swaddled baby.
The wheels jammed on snow ruts as they passed
shop windows full of cakes, books, toys.
Sylvia put down a bruised apple she couldn't afford.
Her little girl insisted she was hungry.
The baby wailed.
The safety pins on his diapers must be cold.
People frowned at the mother
who couldn't keep those children quiet.

In a record-cold January, Sylvia's feet
felt heavy as blocks of ice. The telephone
company had been overbooked all month.
Nothing could be installed in Sylvia's flat.
She parked the pram beside a red and glass
phone booth about the size of a coffin.

Mind your brother, Sylvia told her two-year-old.
Keep your mittens on! She won't.
Under her hood, the little girl cried.
Sylvia wiped her child's nose,
checked numbers she'd scribbled on paper.
She jammed a wool-covered finger into the phone's dial.
Her husband, in bed with another woman, didn't answer.
A friend, and another, were out of their homes.
Her doctor gone for the weekend.

No one heard the ringing,
ringing, ringing. No one answered.

Did Sylvia press her face against the glass panes?
She fed coins until everything was empty.
Her daughter knocked on the glass.
Sylvia couldn't hear her
or the girl at the hotline begging,
Please don't kill yourself.
She couldn't see all the girls opening windows.

Like an Ending

Walking past lilac bushes, I break off a stem,
wave its perfume. Lawns turn deep blue
as breezes shift shadows.
I've almost reached the stationery store
when I see Deborah walking beside a guy
whose trousers aren't baggy around the ankles or hips.
The seams of his jacket align with his shoulders.
Deborah's freshly cut hair curls around her head.
A camel hair coat is belted at her waist.

She nods hello but her gaze shifts to the side
as it did when guys she didn't want to talk to approached.
Maybe she doesn't want to see me
compare this boy to Neil. She's leaving us both.
I'm surprised, but had I just been seeing poorly?
I was proud of her strength but hadn't really listened
to her fear that graduation would mean the end
of food stamps, the check from the state.
The rope we used to toss to each other
–*What are you writing?*–will no longer save.

I'll never know if Claire masters an arabesque
or wobbles on pointe or even took ballet lessons.
As she grows up, will she remember
how clever she was, how brave, and how loved?

Will she read books about goddesses, ordinary girls,
Tess of the d'Urbervilles or Sylvia Plath?
She won't know that I'll always remember her.

PART VII

Bee Colors

Hope and Hiding

I stuff a black gown and flat hat in my bicycle basket,
pedal to the university football field,
find a seat among many rows of metal folding chairs.
I wave a fake diploma, with a real one promised
soon in the mail, whoop and holler congratulations
to myself and thousands of people around me.

A school superintendent interviews me for a job in a city.
She doesn't ask if I vow to wait for girls to raise
their hands even as the arms of eager boys wave. I do.
Instead, her eyes narrow
as she asks about some poor grades
and why it took me so long to finish college.
Memory's weight lessens with time, as I was told
it would, though it took longer than I expected.
I can't tell the truth here, but it hurts
to brush it aside, inside, hint at indecision, laziness.

Still, I get a job teaching in a middle school.
I'll need to drive there. My brother, briefly returning
to Massachusetts, helps me find an old Volkswagen.
When it rains, water splashes through the rusted floor.
The rearview mirror swivels, though I tie it with a bandanna.
I take the car to a service station
where a mechanic twists up a pipe to pump in heat.

I learn Emily Dickinson's grave is behind the shop.

The map with two lines and a triangle wasn't drawn to scale.

My friend and I were on the right street

but assumed more had been left out on paper than was.

Vocation

The classes I teach include some eighth graders
who haven't yet learned to read or write.
Some students are challenged, others smart
but exiled to this wing after brawling with classmates,
threatening teachers, breaking windows.
Every day I pass out books to share,
then collect them, since what leaves the classroom
may never return. I buy packs of multiple pens
which I hand out using the word *borrow*.

Missing pens are the least of the problems.
I've started to look for jobs at other schools
when one afternoon I pick up the mail.
Instead of a note with variations on *Sorry*,
an editor offers to print my story in a small magazine.
To celebrate, I buy a ream of paper,
five hundred blank sheets, and apply
to graduate schools where I can focus on writing.

I choose a university that offers a full scholarship
and a job teaching freshmen English,
then start the summer in the house near the woods.
The professors will travel while I eat off their wooden plates,
watch the dog named after one of Shakespeare's fairies,
and tend to stories. I write because others wrote
before me, because others are writing now.

The Top of a Mountain

Traffic is banned on New York streets where thousands
march shoulder to shoulder protesting nuclear arms.
I walk by a friend's friend whose kind brown eyes are wide.
His shoulders bend as if he's often pulled toward paper.
We chant and yell together, then more quietly talk
about his work illustrating for our local newspaper,
my writing, and the small worlds we want to save.

The next week, we ride bicycles to a mountain.
On the summit, we eat fresh strawberries
Peter brought in a glass jar
so they wouldn't get crushed as he pedaled.
Windblown clouds change
the colors of the river and fields below.
We must be changing, too.
A mountain never stays still. No painter
can keep up with shifting pinks, thickening blues.

Soon, Peter and I meet or talk every day.
His one-room apartment is lined with paperbacks
about elves and wizards, comic books with daredevils,
shapeshifters, mighty heroes, and villains.
Open shelves above the sink hold green glass bowls
and mugs shaped like characters from Star Wars.
A Ouija board he bought secondhand at a yard sale

is the right size to balance between two chair arms,
making a flat surface to hold his pens and ink.

One cool evening back at the house
that's neither mine nor his, we sit by the fireplace.
The old dog sleeps between our feet.
Peter has a deadline for a weekly gardening column
drawing pictures of vegetables or weeds,
sometimes with faces. Across from him,
I write as confidently as I had in second grade,
composing books the size of my hand I let flutter away.

I tell him about the girl I was then and the next year,
taking notes like Harriet the Spy, filling a blue notebook
with poems ending in rhymes or abruptly,
the beginnings of stories, the first acts of plays.
If I could meet that girl
and read those long-gone notebooks,
I wouldn't point out what was good or bad.
I'd take her hands and say, *You can be a writer.*
Or maybe she's always been saying that to me.

Magazines

Peter and I get ice cream in town
one afternoon, talking about what will happen
when I leave soon for grad school. I drove
to New Hampshire to look at bulletin boards
pinned with notices about rooms or roommates,
fringed at the bottom with tear-off phone numbers.
Peter offers to move with me,
but it sounds like too much, too soon.
No matter how much I seek stories
in which a woman has both writing and love,
I don't entirely believe them.
I remind him, *This will be my time to focus on writing.*

He says, *Of course. I'll be working, too.*
Maybe I can send my newspaper assignments
through the mail. And look for freelance jobs.

We stop in the stationery store. I say hello
to old friends and show Peter the magazine
that will publish my story. He declares his love
of this little magazine, then sidesteps
to the section featuring wheeled or flying vehicles.
Thumbing through the smaller array
of literary magazines, my heart thuds
when I spot a new article about Sylvia Plath.

I'm holding this when Peter comes over
with glossier magazines about motorcycles and science.
When I mention Sylvia Plath, his forehead wrinkles.
He says, *She seems kind of intense.*
I don't think art has to come from suffering.

She didn't seek pain. She used writing to cope.
I slip the magazine back on the shelf,
walk past the cash register with empty hands.
Leaving the store, Peter says, *I thought*
you wanted the magazine you showed me.

It cost too much. I feel my face open and split
the way it does when holding back tears.
Because he was ending
what I thought might be love,
because I was ending it, because it was ending.
I tell Peter he should go back
to his own home tonight. I've got work to do.
Deconstructing the small house
I'd been building,
stacking invisible planks and beams.

Across the Room

When I let out the dog the next morning,
I see the magazine I wanted on the stone step.
A glass jelly jar of yellow wildflowers
holds down a note I unfold to a cartoon
Peter drew of two people wearing glasses. Us.
I phone him and say,
I thought you didn't like Sylvia Plath.

Honestly, I don't know much about her,
he says, *but you like her.*

I do. She made mistakes. My voice is too loud
and also shaking. *I like her a lot.*

I ask him to come to the house by the woods.
Orange daylilies lean toward the sun.
As I speak of my damaged heart,
all I'm afraid I may never be, Peter listens.
He offers the curve of his shoulder for my head.

Later, he draws sitting across from me,
the ink-splotched Ouija board
resting on the arms of a stuffed chair.
I pat the dog, open the magazine, take notes
about how Sylvia spent her last days,
the ways we're alike and not alike.
Writing is its own form of survival.

Dark Mornings

Among pale blue, pink, and red-brown buildings,
Sylvia found a flat where Yeats once lived.
Surely that was a sign of rebirth in writing poetry,
though she must climb three flights of stairs
with a baby, toddler, pram, and groceries.
She tacked up a Bruegel print of Icarus falling
as people, sheep, and dogs go about their lives.
Another of noble Isis, shown with wings, in the nursery.
Sylvia lay straw matting in her bedroom,
painted doorframes black: bee colors.

For six weeks, in early morning
before the children opened their eyes,
she rolled paper into her typewriter,
wrote fast, furiously, free
as a wild horse or a goddess riding into daybreak
before hearing the rattle of bottles
left by the milkman, a child's cry.
Sylvia carefully ordered poems in a black binder.
She sewed curtains, but ice coated the windows
during the coldest winter in England
in more than a hundred years.

On her last night, did someone visit or not visit?
Was it just toast for supper, and still it burned?
What if reviews of her novel had been kinder?
If she and the children hadn't come down with flu?

What if the downstairs tenant could hear better
or worse? Maybe he struggled
not to complain about pattering above
as the two-year-old ran back and forth.
What if she'd gotten more sleep?
What if her mother never said, *Pretend it was a dream?*
What if depression didn't carry a hammer and knife?

I turn into the burning wick of a candle, a fist,
furious at her, her estranged husband, her friends,
the distracted doctor, the nurse who arrived too late,
the mother across the ocean.
Everyone who didn't listen when it mattered.

The Last Letter

I'm writing to you, Sylvia. I'm writing to myself.
Early on a February morning,
working in dim light, you set out extra
blankets for the children, buttered bread.
Maybe you couldn't see past your hands
as you poured milk to leave by the cribs.
You opened the nursery windows, though it was cold.
You forced tea towels into the crack under the shut door.
Careful as a carpenter, you pressed tape around the sides,
leaving no gaps, like those in poetry's margins,
where lethal gas might seep in.
You folded a kitchen towel,
rested your head in the oven,
its flame and saving grace shut off.

The home turned almost still till morning.
Waking pigeons flew
past the bare branches of sycamore trees.
The first sound might have been the baby,
enraged when his screams went unanswered.
Near the picture of Isis, the goddess
who helps the dead enter the afterlife,
your little girl may have pounded the door
that wouldn't budge or screamed out the window.

You won't see your boy stack blocks into towers.
You won't hear your daughter
sing about teapots or lambs.
Some people believe you hoped to be saved.
Words give second chances. An oven just one.
Blame or rescue means believing I know better,
instead of listening to how much you hurt.
I'm sorry. Something wrong in your body
broke your sense of belonging to the world.

You couldn't save me. I couldn't save you.
You weren't meant to show me a way to an end
–there are no endings–but to sometimes
stand side by side knocking on windows,
asking for help. Love is glass. Hold it up.
Thank you for what you gave
and for what you couldn't give.
Your poems became rooms I could write in.
I hope mine become places
where someone might breathe for a while.

EPILOGUE

Making My Own Maps

Chances and Claims

I bid goodbye to the unraveling black coat
before Peter and I move to New Hampshire.
I take classes in poetry and fiction, earn a living
teaching composition to university students.
All of them open notebooks. Many write down what I say.

Every evening I sit at my blue typewriter
reaching for a moment when paper seems like glass.
I publish another story, then months later, another.
My public life as a writer is slow, but it's moving,
as I reach toward a chance someone
will see me, themselves, and a bigger world.
To write is to find the courage to claim that we matter.

Cake

For the wedding in our backyard,
I bake a tiered carrot cake that doesn't topple.
Peter carves two triceratopses
bedecked in painted outfits to set on top.

We stay in our shared student house
where late one night, Peter and a friend
pass sketchbooks back and forth, laughing.
They begin to write, draw, and self-publish
a comic book about four turtles, brothers
who bumble to mastery of the martial arts.
We wonder if the cartons stacked
in the dining room will sell. By the time
I earn a writing degree and teach
high school for two years, the comic
is successful enough–Cowabunga!–
that I can throw away my grade books
and lesson plans. A few years later,
I become a mother who writes.

What's Saved

Over the years I publish poems about women
who were famous in their day for painting,
exploring the sea, peering through microscopes,
then forgotten. In libraries and archives, I track down
ruler-straight fact, then imagine my way into the gaps
between sometimes dull, sometimes astonishing work.
I want to make something whole, though life rambles.
A poem is not life, but something that might change one.

All these many years later, the wooden table
where I wrote my first good stories
stands in the basement.
On top are cartons of papers, a long-broken microwave.
My typewriter has been traded for a laptop,
but on my desk an old blue mug
holds pens by found feathers, pine cones,
colored leaves that turn dry, fragile, and pale.
I write so something isn't lost.
Building a place where I can live,
like the houses I forged as a child
out of shoeboxes or under trees,
scraping pine needles into low, roofless walls.

Today

Apples fill a bowl. The black dog is sleeping.
These things will change, too. Fruit and naps don't last.
Like ghosts, poems don't have true ends.
A final page is not a thudding door, but disappearance,
quiet as a bird becoming part of the sky again.

A Few More Words from the Author

Thank you for reading, which takes courage. Together, readers and writers can make words come alive, offering new chances for change.

Knocking on Windows is a verse memoir, shaped by events and spoken sentences that long stayed with me as a base to develop scenes. Memories change each time they're pulled up, making a layered art, like a collage. Memory shows up in bursts and crosses with imagination, shifting shine, dipping into shadows. While my poems start in fact and I tried to follow calendars, I compressed time to highlight connections and followed poetry's call for rhythm, unity, and believability wrought by detail. The texture of language sets its own truths.

I left out or showed only glimpses of the many people who have made my life better, but I'm thankful for too many people to name. My aim was to show between two covers the patterns of struggle and hope, a sense of my life as a reader and writer.

One Girl's Introduction to Literature

We are made partly of the books, myths, fairy tales, and poems we read, memorize, skim, or leave on shelves. I offer thanks to many, including the following (in order of the work's publication):

"Mary Had a Little Lamb" by Sarah Josepha Hale (1830)

The Scarlet Letter by Nathaniel Hawthorne (1850)

Moby Dick by Herman Melville (1851)

Little Women by Louisa May Alcott (1868)

Poems by Emily Dickinson (1890)

Tess of the d'Urbervilles by Thomas Hardy (1891)

"Spring and Fall" by Gerard Manley Hopkins (1918)
Márgarét, áre you grieving Over Goldengrove unleaving?

"The Second Coming" by William Butler Yeats (1920)
Turning and turning in the widening gyre.

"Paterson" by William Carlos Williams (1927)
No ideas but in things.

Native Son by Richard Wright (1940)

"Musée des Beaux Arts" by W. H. Auden (1940)
*. . . the expensive delicate ship that must have seen
Something amazing, a boy falling out of the sky, Had
somewhere to get to and sailed calmly on.*

The Diary of Anne Frank by Anne Frank (1947)
I still believe, in spite of everything, that people are really good at heart.

Howl and Other Poems by Allen Ginsburg (1956)

On the Road by Jack Kerouac (1957)

The Elements of Style by William Strunk Jr. with E. B. White (1959)
Prefer the specific to the general . . . the concrete to the abstract.

Lunch Poems by Frank O'Hara (1964)

Harriet the Spy by Louise Fitzhugh (1964)

Ariel by Sylvia Plath (1965)

I Know Why the Caged Bird Sings by Maya Angelou (1969)

The Bell Jar by Sylvia Plath (1971)

"*The Ambition Bird*" by Anne Sexton (1972)
All night dark wings flopping in my heart.
Each an ambition bird.

"*Vincent*" by Don McLean (1972)

Through My Eyes by Ruby Bridge (1999)

Red Comet: The Short Life and Blazing Art of Sylvia Plath by Heather Clark (2020)